Irving Babbitt

Twayne's United States Authors Series

Kenneth E. Eble, Editor

University of Utah

TUSAS 518

IRVING BABBITT
(1865–1933)
Photograph reproduced courtesy of the Babbitt family.

Irving Babbitt

By Stephen C. Brennan
and Stephen R. Yarbrough

Texas A&M University

Twayne Publishers
A Division of G. K. Hall & Co. • *Boston*

Irving Babbitt

Stephen C. Brennan
Stephen R. Yarbrough

Copyright © 1987 by G.K. Hall & Co.
All Rights Reserved
Published by Twayne Publishers
A Division of G.K. Hall & Co.
70 Lincoln Street
Boston, Massachusetts 02111

Copyediting supervised by Lewis DeSimone
Book production by Janet Zietowski
Book design by Barbara Anderson

Typeset in 11 pt. Garamond
by Modern Graphics, Inc., Weymouth, Massachusetts

Printed on permanent/durable acid-free paper
and bound in the United States of America

Library of Congress Cataloging in Publication Data

Brennan, Stephen C.
    Irving Babbit.

    (Twayne's United States authors series ; TUSAS 518)
    Bibliography: p.
    Includes index.
    1. Babbitt, Irving, 1865–1933.   2. Humanism—
History—20th century.   I. Yarbrough, Stephen R.
II. Title.   III. Series.
B945.B124B74   1987   191   87–420
ISBN 0–8057–7499–8

Contents

About the Authors
Preface
Acknowledgments
Chronology

Chapter One
From Romance to Ritual: A Humanist's Conversion   1

Chapter Two
A Philosophy of Disciplined Choice   28

Chapter Three
The Humanist Campaign   58

Chapter Four
Humanist Literary Theory   79

Chapter Five
Humanism and the Psychology
of Education and Politics   103

Chapter Six
Humanism and Religion   129

Notes and References   143
Selected Bibliography   157
Index   162

About the Authors

Stephen R. Yarbrough received his Ph.D. in Modern Thought and Literature from Pennsylvania State University (1982). He was a Fellow of the School for Criticism and Theory at Northwestern University (1982) and a National Endowment for the Humanities Interdisciplinary Fellow (1975–76). Presently an assistant professor of English at Texas A&M University, he has published articles on Jonathan Edwards (*Journal of the History of Ideas*), Emerson and Thoreau (*Thoreau Journal Quarterly*), Charles Brockden Brown (*Studies in American Fiction*), structuralist theory (*New Orleans Review*), poststructuralist theory (*South Central Review*), and postmodern humanism (*Man and World*).

Stephen C. Brennan, also an assistant professor of English at Texas A&M University, earned his Ph.D. in American literature at Tulane University, which he attended on a National Defense Education Act Fellowship. Before coming to Texas A&M, he taught for three years at Drexel University in Philadelphia. He has published articles on Browning (*Studies in Browning and His Circle*) and Dreiser (*The Dreiser Newsletter, Research Studies,* and *American Literary Realism, 1870–1910*).

Preface

Irving Babbitt, a professor of French and comparative literature at Harvard University during the first three decades of this century, was a man of great purpose. He wanted to save, not the world, but the few, to save them from those who wanted to save the world and to save them from themselves. He was the acknowledged founder and leader of what came to be known as the "New Humanism." His primary aim for this movement was to convince others that powerful forces—biological, psychological, and social—worked against the freedom of the spirit. These forces deprived the individual of the ability to deliberate and choose, making life aimless, without purpose, not truly human. To this extent his beliefs corresponded to the deterministic modes of thought found in Calvinist religion, Freudian psychology, Darwinian biology, Huxlian sociology. Unlike the determinists, however, Babbitt believed that freedom and dignity could be wrested from these forces through the individual's assertion of what he called the "higher will"—the human capacity to imagine and choose a controlling purpose, to refuse to act upon impulses that contradicted that purpose, and continually to test the validity of the purpose itself.

Babbitt believed that such ethical freedom was possible only for the individual, that concern for classes or special interest groups was the death of liberty. He therefore opposed what he called "humanitarians"—Marxists, socialists, utilitarian reformers of all kinds—accusing them of shifting the responsibility for ethical action from themselves onto social groups. Still, Babbitt saw enough truth in determinism to distrust profoundly the ability of individuals to set their own goals. An individual who follows intuition forfeits a necessary critical distance. Goals must be taken from the "outside" and be tested against not only one's personal experience but also against the experience of the past, the tradition. Thus, in addition to the determinists and the humanitarians, Babbitt opposed all those who trusted some kind of "inner oracle," including transcendentalists, expressionists, religious mystics—even some pragmatists.

Since he unsparingly attacked others' ideas, since his beliefs cut so sharply across the grain of contemporary opinion, attitudes toward

Babbitt were, and still are, often as uncompromising as the principles he stood for. He has been called a saint and a degenerate, a rebel and a reactionary, a prophet and a fool. His students, however, agree upon at least one thing: Babbitt was a great teacher. If a teacher is to be judged by the greatness of his students—the list includes T. S. Eliot, Stuart Sherman, Harry Levin, Austin Warren, Van Wyck Brooks, Norman Foerster, and Walter Lippmann—Babbitt was indeed, as Eliot once called him, "the master."

Babbitt was not, unfortunately, a great writer. Too obviously, his books were derived from classroom lectures. And while his published work exhibits the strengths of the inspirational teacher— well-turned phrases, ample and just illustrations—it lacks the clear exposition of ideas, the precise definitions, and the sharply drawn lines between the abstract concept and the particular opinion that one expects of an important philosopher or critic. Babbitt does have a well-developed, original philosophical position and a corresponding critical method, but the exposition of both the position and the method is scattered in fragments across five books and two collections of essays. Even the one essay that attempts to summarize the principles of his humanism, "What I Believe," is too vague and thus likely to be misleading to anyone who has not assimilated the rest of his work.

As one might expect, this unsystematic quality of Babbitt's writing has led to distorted interpretations of his thought, this and the fact that most of these interpretations have been undertaken from points of view alien to Babbitt's own. Although scholarly work on Babbitt has increased recently in both quantity and quality, culminating in Thomas R. Nevin's *Irving Babbitt: An Intellectual Study* (1984), as of today there exists neither a full-length biography nor a sustained analysis of his philosophy and its relationship to his theories of literary criticism, education, religion, and politics. The ambition of the present critical biography is to fill, at least partially, both of these voids as concisely as possible. It attempts to define the basic principles of Babbitt's humanism, retrieving them from the context of his private experience and the social, intellectual, and political climate as Babbitt himself saw it, in order to explain more clearly how his thought should be understood within the context of our own time. To these ends, the authors have presented as much previously unpublished primary material as possible and have, with some exceptions, analyzed his work as a whole rather than book by book.

Some of the difficulty today's readers have in gauging Babbitt's present relevance to philosophical and critical problems arises from his tone: his trenchant divisions between right and wrong, his tendency to use the word *feminine* pejoratively, his disparagement of almost all things modern, his devaluation of nearly every major writer the Western world has produced—such attitudes make it difficult for anyone to take him seriously at first. He often reminds one of an old politician whose party has not won an election in twenty years, sitting on a park bench, babbling about the good old days. And, in a sense, he was. Babbitt did feel very much alienated from his society's values. But such a picture is a caricature, not a portrait. One of the primary intentions of the present volume is to restore Babbitt's own perspective to a reading of his work, to make his particular angle of vision evident for the present.

In so doing, this critical biography will argue that many of Babbitt's attitudes which readers find so dated Babbitt himself would not assume today. He believed that critical judgments should be dated, that a critic should counterbalance prevailing tendencies—should lean to the right when society leans to the left, should move inward when society moves outward. This belief follows from humanism's first law, the law of measure. Like his German contemporary Martin Heidegger, Babbitt felt sharply the finitude of man. Being finite, human beings cannot attain to Truth, only to half-truths, and for every half-truth there is an equal and opposite countertruth. People tend to take a half-truth for the whole truth and to follow its implications toward infinity. Babbitt calls this tendency in philosophy monism; in politics and religion, fanaticism. Such tendencies necessarily lead to destruction. The critic's task is to mediate these opposing tendencies, and the humanistic standard is the perfect reconciliation of all opposites—not the halfway measures, the middle-of-the-road compromises of middle-class liberality but the affirmation of the equality of the extremes and the active prevention of the one's dominating or subverting the other.

Babbitt knew that his form of humanism emerged only rarely in Western literature, even more rarely as the norm in Western society, though more commonly in the East. He measured the history of civilization in terms of its eras' divergences from and approximations toward the humanistic standard. He saw his own era as an extreme divergence, and he was not surprised that his contemporaries viewed his own opinions as extreme. Babbitt remains perhaps the most neglected and misunderstood important American thinker of the twentieth century. The authors hope that this volume will contribute toward restoring, if not his influence, at least his own point of view, so that his unusual position may be judged more fairly.

Stephen C. Brennan
Stephen R. Yarbrough

Texas A&M University

Acknowledgments

For whatever success they might have had in explaining the thought of an important American literary and social critic, the authors owe a debt of gratitude to many. Texas A&M graduate students Marlea Hawkins and Keith Waddle offered valuable research assistance during the early stages of this project. In the spring and summer of 1985 the College of Liberal Arts at Texas A&M helped greatly by reducing teaching loads and by funding research in the Babbitt Papers at Harvard University. For two weeks during that summer, the staff of the Harvard University Archives made one of the authors feel less a stranger and helped him find his way through the seeming chaos of Babbitt's papers. Several persons served as checks on the authors' expansive impulses by reading the manuscript in various stages and offering much needed editorial advice—Jeffrey N. Cox, Adelaide P. McGinnis, Robert D. Newman, Lawrence J. Oliver, David H. Stewart, and Bonnie Yarbrough. Finally, special thanks are due Edward S. Babbitt, not only for his great generosity in allowing the authors access to his father's papers at Harvard and to many other papers heretofore in the family's possession, but for his hospitality and his willingness to share his memories during a visit to his home in South Hadley, Massachusetts.

Chronology

1865	Born in Dayton, Ohio, 2 August.
ca. 1866	The family moves to New York, where his father teaches penmanship.
ca. 1869	With his brother and mother, goes to live with his maternal grandparents on a farm near Madisonville, Ohio.
ca. 1871	The family reunites in New York.
ca. 1873	Returns to Ohio with his mother, brother, and sister.
ca. 1875	The family again reunites in New York, where Irving's father has become a magnetist and psycho-physician.
1876	Returns to the Madisonville farm with his brother, mother, and sister.
1877	His mother dies. His brother heads west, leaving Irving to help on the farm.
1881	Qualifies to teach in the Hamilton County, Ohio, public schools, but his father and new stepmother arrive and buy a home in a Cincinnati suburb. Attends Woodward High School and begins classical studies.
1884	Spends the summer on the Wyoming ranch managed by his uncle.
1885	After high school graduation, works as a newspaper reporter. Enters Harvard in the fall.
1887–1888	Takes his junior year off for a fifteen-month walking tour of Europe.
1889	Graduates with honors in classics from Harvard. Takes a job teaching classics at the College of Montana in Deer Lodge.
1891–1892	Studies Sanskrit and Pali under Sylvain Lévi in Paris.
1892–1893	Takes his A.M. at Harvard. Meets Paul Elmer More and studies Dante under Charles Eliot Norton.

1893–1894	Teaches Romance languages at Williams College.
1894	Hired as instructor in Harvard's French Department.
1897	Publishes his first scholarly article, "The Rational Study of the Classics," in the *Atlantic Monthly*.
1900	Teaches his first advanced course at Harvard. Marries Dora Drew.
1901	Daughter Esther born.
1902	Promoted to assistant professor. Begins teaching classes in the Comparative Literature Department.
1903	Son Edward born.
1908	*Literature and the American College.*
1910	*The New Laokoon.*
1912	Promoted to full professor and given tenure. *The Masters of Modern French Criticism.*
1919	*Rousseau and Romanticism.*
1920	Elected to the National Institute of Arts and Letters.
1923	Teaches at the Sorbonne as an exchange professor.
1924	*Democracy and Leadership.*
1926	Becomes a corresponding member of the French Institute (*Académie des Sciences Morales et Politiques*).
1930	Debates Henry Seidel Canby and Carl Van Doren at Carnegie Hall. Contributes to the humanist manifesto *Humanism and America*. Elected to the American Academy of Arts and Letters.
1932	*On Being Creative.* Receives an honorary Doctor of Humane Letters degree from Bowdoin College.
1933	Dies at his Cambridge home 15 July.

Chapter One

From Romance to Ritual: A Humanist's Conversion

For almost forty years, Irving Babbitt, the "Warring Buddha of Harvard" and leader of a group popularly known as the "New Humanists," relentlessly denounced modern culture as a horrible jumble of scientific determinism and romantic sentimentalism and espoused the classical ideals of decorum and the golden mean. He distrusted human nature and despised utopian schemes; civilization's survival, he held, required an equivalent for Christian grace, a doctrine losing its power to restrain the individual's expansive desires and aggressive instincts. From his days as a Harvard graduate student in the early 1890s until his death in 1933, he expressed these beliefs so consistently that even Paul Elmer More, his closest friend and fellow humanist, found "something almost inhuman in the immobility of his central ideas." To More, his friend seemed to have "sprung up, like Minerva, fully grown and fully armed," and even today he strikes some commentators as simply a "born conservative." As a result, Babbitt has always seemed to stand just outside of progressive, democratic American life. H. L. Mencken detected in his diatribes against modernism "a faint perfume of [a] college town society" unable to appreciate "the whole, gross, glittering, excessively dynamic, infinitely grotesque, incredibly stupendous drama of American life." But to a disciple like Austin Warren, Babbitt's disaffection was simply that of the New England saint, "to whom reality was the spiritual life."[1]

Babbitt was not a born conservative: his early life strongly affected his later views, and his creed approached its final form only in his late twenties, after his conversion from his earlier, typically American, and contradictory beliefs. He frequently called for a similar conversion in others, for a redirection of expansive energy toward inner unity and what he termed "centrality." As George A. Panichas has remarked, Babbitt's paramount spiritual need was to "connect and unify the inner life and the outer life."[2]

Like most midwesterners coming of age after the Civil War, he lacked this unity; outwardly, he emulated the rugged individualists who were conquering the wilderness while inwardly he idealized the genteel, mannered, and literary New England Brahmins. In terms of nineteenth-century perceptions of gender, he suffered from a conflict between his masculine and feminine sides, for the active, practical life had become the masculine domain, while "culture" had become sentimentalized and given over almost entirely to women and "feminine" men. As Ann Douglas has concluded, American culture during the years of Babbitt's boyhood "seemed bent on establishing a perpetual Mother's Day" and literature "was functioning more and more as . . . a complicated mass dream-life in the busiest, most wide-awake society in the world."[3] Babbitt wanted to unify the nation's psyche—and his own—by reclaiming culture as a masculine pursuit. When Mencken thought he caught a whiff of perfume in Babbitt's defense of culture and decorum, he showed his obtuseness. Babbitt was not trying to impose an effete, "feminized" culture on America; he was trying to invigorate that culture, restore its active influence on practical life, save it from women and prissy dilettantes, and thereby keep civilization from degenerating into barbarism.

Today's readers are thus likely to read Babbitt as a militant sexist. In this at least, he does not stand apart from his age. He would not have relished the comparison, but the creed he formulated in the 1890s, like Jack London's celebration of the "great blond beast" and Teddy Roosevelt's chest-thumping imperialism, asserted masculinity in what seemed an overly refined and too highly civilized society. He decried all forms of naturalism and imperialism, yet his first book, *Literature and the American College* (1908), called for "a resolute and manly grappling with the plain facts of existence" and thus contributed to what has come to be known as "the strenuous age."[4]

Cowboys, Angels, and Delicate Fancies

Irving Babbitt's family roots reached deep into the stern Puritan culture of New England. His grandfather (a graduate of Yale Divinity School) and great-grandfather (a graduate of Harvard) had been Congregationalist ministers upholding the tradition of a learned clergy against evangelical fervor and rampant anti-intellectualism.

A respect for learning and culture was thus an important part of Irving's heritage. His father, Edwin Babbitt, attended Knox College in Galesburg, Illinois, and taught school for several years before founding the Miami Commercial College in Dayton, Ohio, in 1860. Irving was born in Dayton on 2 August 1865, a few months after Appomattox. He was the second of three children, six years younger than brother Tom and five years older than sister Katherine. His mother, Augusta Darling Babbitt, was a frail, gentle woman who apparently left no lasting impression on her younger son. His father's influence, however, was great. In many ways an epitome of nineteenth-century American attitudes, Edwin represented everything Irving came to despise.

Infected by the country's postwar expansive optimism, the elder Babbitt was a man on the make. Unfortunately, none of his schemes panned out, and he could never provide his family security or stability. Before Irving was a year old, Edwin uprooted the family and headed east to Brooklyn. There he sold stationery supplies and taught penmanship (he had published *The Babbittonian System of Penmanship* in 1863). After about three years of hard times, he had to send Gussie, Tom, and Irving to live at the Darling farm outside Madisonville, Ohio. When Irving was six, and again when he was about nine, Edwin reunited the family in New York, but each time, after struggling a year or two, he had to send his wife and children back to Ohio.

During this last period in New York in the mid-1870s, Augusta had to take in boarders, Tom had to work in a wholesale glassware store for three dollars a week, and Irving had to sell newspapers. These experiences may explain why Irving later exhausted himself by lecturing widely and teaching extra courses while paradoxically calling for a life of meditative leisure. And the instability of these early years undoubtedly planted the seeds of his later reverence for order.

When Irving was eleven and living in Ohio, his mother died. Tom headed to Texas to punch cattle, while Irving was left to help around the farm. Grandfather Lucius Darling, an ex-schoolteacher, encouraged Irving to study, so that in the spring of 1881, when he was just fifteen, he passed the examination qualifying him to teach in the Hamilton County public schools. He might have spent his days in one-room Ohio schoolhouses but for his father, who showed up with a new wife—a heartbroken widow with twenty thousand dollars. Stepmother Bessie bought a house in the Walnut Hills section of Cincinnati, and the fall of 1881 found Irving and his sister living with their father and stepmother (whose own children had all died).

This new life was hardly idyllic. By 1885, Edwin was back in New York making excuses for not sending money. According to Irving's cousin Sadie, Bessie was "very trying. . . . I remember hearing her say she 'broke the wills of *her* children,' & I thought, no wonder they all died." Nevertheless, Cincinnati, a midwestern cultural center, gave Irving his first real taste of life among respectable, cultured young ladies and gentlemen. More important, at Woodward High School he had an excellent classics teacher who helped him gain fair fluency in Greek and Latin and introduced him to the Horatian virtues of grace and decorum. By his senior year, he was set on going to elitist Harvard, perhaps in part because Edwin taught him to view Boston as "our real Athens" and to admire Bostonians for their ability to attain "elegance & culture . . . better than anybody else."[5]

Irving nearly didn't get to Harvard. Just before graduating from Woodward in the spring of 1885, near the top of his class, he and his stepmother had a serious argument, perhaps because he turned down a scholarship to Kenyon College (which could have led to a teaching job at Kenyon Grammar School) to gamble on the more prestigious Eastern university. Moving into a dingy Cincinnati attic apartment, Irving took a job as a reporter for a newspaper. As a consequence, he missed the three-day Harvard entrance examinations given at Cincinnati in June. To get into Harvard, he would have to scrape up tuition money and pass the entrance examinations in Cambridge just before classes started in September. Fortunately, his uncle Albert in Wyoming and his uncle Thomas in Dayton came up with the money. In September he went East, passed the entrance examinations, and found himself among the scions of Brahmin stock.

The twenty-year-old freshman held a curious mixture of attitudes shaped by his early experiences in Ohio and New York. The geographical distance between the two places was not great, but to young Irving they must have seemed like different planets.

At the Darling farm, grandfather Lucius, in contrast to father Edwin, was a model of discipline and hard work. Until crippled in his last years, Mr. Darling was a strong, vigorous man who always maintained an ex-schoolteacher's authority. He was the family patriarch who took in and supported a divorced daughter with several children, as well as the Babbitts.

Perhaps a more important influence was Irving's older brother Tom and the other boys on the farm. In those days rural boys had to earn their way into a closed male society hostile to their parents' "feminine" values of conformity and good manners—often with their fists. The boys' gang was a vestige of frontier life and, with its loyalties and sense of rough male justice, resembled the comitatus of the heroic age. For many men in the late nineteenth century, initiation into the boys' gang seemed a necessary step toward practical success.[6]

Irving probably had a tough time winning his way into the comitatus. He was a slender, feminine-looking boy with none-too-robust health. He spent much of his time reading, and when he went to fetch his grandfather's newspapers, his cousin Stephen Mahon frequently had to hunt for him, always finding him reading under a tree. Such a boy, unless he continually asserted his manhood, would be labeled a pantywaist. No one, Irving decided early in life, would pin that label on him. His stories about his youth always centered on displays of male prowess, such as the time he and the other boys accidentally drank hard cider and only he managed not to get sick and the times he handled himself against street bullies in New York. He developed a swagger and an air of self-confidence that earned the "awe" of his little cousin Sadie.[7]

Even when studying the classics at Woodward High and planning to attend Harvard, he envied his brother Tom's life in the Wild West. Although he joined the local Washington Irving Literary Society, playing the dandy to attract young ladies with cultural pretensions, he was an uncomfortable aesthete. Like Teddy Roosevelt, he headed West to prove his manhood. In the summer of 1884 he visited the ranch his Uncle Albert Babbitt managed near Cheyenne, Wyoming. At first, he had so much fun that he thought about joining Tom in Texas. When Tom responded with a dreary account of life "riding these confounded broncos," dealing with "desperate and unprincipled" men, and battling malaria,[8] and when life in Wyoming turned out to involve nights in vermin-infested cabins and monotonous rides on cattle trains, Irving soon gave up dreams of becoming a real cowboy. Nevertheless, this summer was his life's great adventure, and even when many considered him a representative New Englander he loved to recount how he pulled a

rattlesnake out of its hole by the tail, how he was attacked by an
eagle, and how he narrowly escaped a flash flood. But he was perhaps
proudest of the "handle" he earned from one of the cowboys—"The
Long Kid."

Above all, Irving's life in the Midwest and his summer in Wyoming fueled his yearning for male camaraderie. As a Harvard sophomore who had yet to embrace the aristocratic principle, he celebrated
the "pure, unadulterated democracy of a cow-camp" where "associate
in absolute equality graduates of Harvard . . . and men who cannot
write their own names." And he wrote joyously of "the wild gal[l]ops
of the round-up by day" and "the frolic and song and story around
the camp-fire of the bivouac at night."[9] These attitudes seem strange
in a young man determined to educate himself in the most elite
college in America, but they are understandable in light of his deep
ambivalence toward his father, who represented an intolerably "feminine" version of the learning and culture Irving loved.

Edwin was not just a bad provider; he was an ineffectual man
who contributed to his son's lifelong distaste for weakness and emotional display. In that difficult summer of 1885, when Irving badly
needed money to go to Harvard, Edwin could only beg forgiveness
for letting him down:

I am straining every possible nerve to do the part of a father to you which
you so raspingly accuse me of not doing. . . . You find vastly more fault
with me than I do with you, & a stranger might think you the father &
I the son by the way you bring me up standing. Your rasping remark
about all my 'absurd' statements that you would not waste time and paper
in answering was not true . . . for what I said about the law & its
imperfections did not apply to law as it now is, but to . . . a system of
things that ought to be.[10]

Although the context of their dispute is not clear, Irving was plainly
bitter that while Edwin mooned over what ought to be, he had to
struggle with the facts of existence.

Edwin's emotional castration may have increased Irving's respect
for his Calvinist forebears. Edwin taught his son to hate Calvinism's
harsh doctrines, yet Irving always admired the Puritans' awe before
a Father whose arbitrary Will orders the creation. The decline of
the Puritan ethic, he would argue, caused the American family's
disintegration, a disintegration he had known firsthand. Lacking a
father he could look up to and rejecting the Father of Christian

dogma, Irving would seek the equivalent in the humanist sages—Buddha, Confucius, Socrates—and in what he would call the "higher self" which all men possess in common.

Irving's distaste for his father would eventually extend to most of the beliefs that Edwin embraced after rejecting Calvinism. In the late 1860s, a lonely failure in New York feeling the gloomy doctrines of predestination and innate depravity weighing upon him "like an incubus," Edwin attended a séance. He soon converted to Spiritualism, a hodgepodge of nineteenth-century American attitudes. Like most Spiritualists, he embraced the facile optimism of the American Transcendentalists. Man is "absolutely divine," the spirits assured him; there is no evil: "all suffering is either remedial, helping us to repent of wrong doing, or acts as a discipline to strengthen us or develop in us the beautiful quality of sympathy for others." Onto this half-baked Emersonianism, Edwin grafted a radical belief in infinite progress derived from Swedenborg's mystical vision of concentric spiritual spheres. The future holds endless cycles of world-building: "the deific activities having reached an utmost verge of the universe, beyond which it will never go, there is a still more wonderful and sublime series of activities and evolutions working up all worlds and all beings into that which is more refined and beautiful."[11] In contrast to the inner calm and peace Irving would define as happiness, Edwin's eternity offered only the frenzied external activity characteristic of American life.

Edwin was also a sentimentalist. He filled the books he began to write with pictures of ethereal women and young girls to illustrate his ideals of purity and spiritual aspiration and thus seems to fit the image many critics had of Spiritualists. Mediums had to surrender their own wills to the spirits, and therefore were often scorned as weak and "feminine." As one hostile minister asserted, a medium must be "in a negative passive condition, of a nervous temperament with cold hands, of a mild, impressible, and gentle disposition. Hence girls and females make the best mediums." Although not a woman, Edwin expressed many sentiments his age would have judged unmanly, as in his daily prayer to God (an androgynous "infinite Father-Spirit and Mother-Spirit of all Life"): "Help me to love thee supremely for thou art supremely lovely, and help me to feel and care for thy dear human children. . . ."[12] When Irving came East to New York as a boy fresh from the farm, he thus found himself in what must have seemed a disturbingly feminine environment

associated with a shabby, disreputable existence on the fringes of
society.

Edwin's turn to Spiritualism was hardly an isolated phenomenon.
Between 1850 and the late 1870s millions of Americans who had
lost their faith in revealed religion dabbled with Spiritualism because, surprisingly, it appealed to their naive faith in science. Spirit
rappings, floating tables, and levitating mediums were passed off
as scientific evidence of an afterlife. Spirits, it was argued, were not
mysterious; they were merely refined forms of matter living in worlds
very much like this one. [13]

It is not surprising, then, that Edwin's spiritualism involved a
pseudoscientific faith in all sorts of "fine forces"—heat, light, mag-
netism, electricity. In the early 1870s he set up in Chicago and
Boston as a "magnetist" and "psychophysician," though his specialty
would become "Chromo-Therapeutics," the application of colored
light for its supposed health benefits. When the family joined him
in New York City in 1874 or 1875, he was listing himself as a
physician and publisher, and during the next several years Babbitt
and Company turned out a series of Edwin's books, among them
The Health Guide: Aiming at a Higher Science of Life and the Life-Forces
(1874), *The Principles of Light and Color: Including among Other Things
the Harmonic Laws of the Universe . . . and the General Philosophy of
Fine Forces* (1878), and *Religion as Revealed by the Material and Spiritual
Universe* (1881). Edwin also began marketing a series of gadgets for
applying colors—colored lampshades, colored flasks, even a pat-
ented contraption resembling a sweatbox for bathing in colored
light.

In denying a duality of spirit and matter, Edwin and the other
Spiritualists were disguised naturalists who committed the error
Irving would find in all forms of monism: absolving the individual
of moral responsibility. "The material and spiritual," Edwin maintained, "are simply the two poles of the same immeasurable scale
of being and both subject to the same laws of chemical action." If
ministers devoted themselves to "the upbuilding of man through
physical laws . . . they could bring about a salvation of human
beings based on fundamental principles." Vice and crime were physical diseases; he himself had often cured licentiousness "by influencing the occiput and lower spine" with heat and diet. [14] To use
Irving's characteristic phrasing derived from Emerson, Edwin replaced "law for man" with "law for thing."

Finally, Edwin was an altruist who wanted to perfect "both the material and spiritual universe." Irving would feel only contempt for those who wanted to perfect the world before they perfected themselves. In every sentimental humanitarian he saw his father's saintly face—or rather the saintly mask of the con artist impotent to express a deep-seated desire for power. Edwin was always after the fast buck, after some key to unlock the door to wealth and prestige. Unable to attract wealthy patients, he had to project his dream of success into the afterlife. In this world, he confessed, gentle and polished men might be pushed aside by those with powerful intellects and wills; however, power increases as the spirit rises "into a condition of love, purity, and high aspiration." In the spirit world *"refinement* is the law of power."[15]

Irving would argue again and again that the twin evils of scientific and sentimental humanitarianism were the loathed spawn of Bacon and Rousseau. But his antipathy toward these evils sprang directly from his painfully embarrassing experiences with his own father. Trusting in man's goodness and natural sympathy and believing in endless progress through the control of nature, Edwin Babbitt combined the two naturalistic streams that eroded a humane civilization, and his idealism masked the crassest of commercial motives. Irving would later be accused of endlessly "shadow-boxing with the ghost of Jean-Jacques Rousseau," who reminded him of "a high-strung impressionable woman" preferring "to a world of sharp definition a world of magic and suggestiveness."[16] But he was also struggling with the ghost of Edwin Babbitt.

Irving's intense hatred of humanitarianism was probably due to his own youthful acceptance of his father's beliefs; no one is more righteous than the convert. Although the Irving Babbitt who went off to Cambridge seemed a brash westerner who looked a man in the eye and spoke without regard for parlor formalities, he as yet maintained what he would later consider the romantic's feminine and sentimental attitude toward culture. One of his high school essays in the Harvard Archives, "Mistakes of the Ancients," while criticizing the Greeks for lacking that go-getter American spirit found in "the hum of factory and workshop, and in the bustle of the crowded mart," argued that America needed more of the "poetry of life" and the Greeks' appreciation for "the delicate fancies of literature and art." Although already committed to the "just mean," he conceived of it only as the opposition of incompatible extremes and not the humanistic mediation of extremes.

Irving owed his father at least one positive intellectual debt—a wide-ranging curiosity and a desire to search out the essential shared truths of the world's great religions. Edwin aspired to be a "true freeman in philosophy and religion," one who practices "a genuine cosmopolitan eclecticism, [and] lovingly grasps the truths of all inspirations, all bibles, all sciences." He believed the Golden Rule to be the essence of religion and concluded that Buddhists, Muslims, and Hindus surpass Christians in sympathy and charity. He particularly admired Buddhism, for its five rules of conduct have "a wider application in the daily affairs of human life" than the Christian Ten Commandments. At Harvard and in his studies abroad Irving would eventually find a different truth in these religions—the need for restraint—but his own eclecticism and reverence for Oriental thought owe much to his father's example. [17]

Undergraduate Days

The Long Kid and Assistant Professor Babbitt.   Irving did not fit in at Harvard. His classmates found his clothes too bohemian, his Western frankness offensive, and his background less than respectable, if not downright vulgar. William Giese, then his closest friend, says Irving in those days professed a "startlingly crude supernaturalism" and told stories of having seen tables and pianos floating in the air; he even took Giese to see a noted Boston medium, though the woman's husband turned them away. Irving may have been having fun with his friend, for he had a westerner's outrageous sense of humor (as a bored Cincinnati reporter he had planted a phony account of a friend's ghastly suicide). Yet when a New York medium gave Edwin an unflattering character reading of his son, the angry freshman seriously accused his father of telepathic fraud. "You say," Edwin replied in denying the charge, "Mr. Dawborn read my mind in describing you. . . ."[18]

In his room in College House ("a horrid dormitory on the noisy and bustling Harvard Square") Irving would read the classics for their "strange and intangible charm" and daydream, forming, "in imagination, the man of Greece or Rome."[19] As a sophomore he moved into a room off campus and was even more of a loner.

Outside his room he projected a different personality. He struck Giese with his "earnest expression," "nonchalant gait," and "visible unconcern with any dandiacal pretensions." He would intrude himself into trivial conversations and assault others' romantic notions with "irrepressible militancy." If anyone objected to his violent attacks, he responded, "I am not thin-skinned . . . and I do not readily adjust myself to people who are." Such external aggressiveness combined with a deep reluctance to share his inner life brought many acquaintances but few intimates. He still professed an adolescent aversion to girls and showed little respect for his polished and learned professors. Giese first saw Irving at Harvard sitting "in solitary prominence" in the front row of a freshman Greek class and so baiting the young Ph.D. with recondite questions that the Long Kid was soon being referred to, somewhat derisively, as "Assistant Professor Babbitt."[20]

It took him seventeen years to become Assistant Professor Babbitt in fact, and by that time the rough edges had been nearly smoothed away. However, no amount of Cambridge culture would ever completely disguise the Long Kid, whose hair-trigger wit and irrepressible militancy were likely to show themselves at any time. The problem for sophomore Babbitt was to make this masculine personality something more than a protective mask for the romantic dreamer.

Go east young man. In 1929 Babbitt said that by the time he graduated from Harvard he had "developed humanistic convictions not unlike those I still hold."[21] The mature creed, though, was several years away. These college years were a time of assimilation and, more important, orientation—in a literal sense. For until he turned intellectually toward the Orient, and the classical culture that had flourished at the meeting place of the Orient and Occident, he was just a confused college boy who had read many books.

His sophomore year was critical. He had come to Harvard with no clear plans, though in addition to the classics he had studied engineering and bookkeeping in high school and his family had encouraged him to pursue some such practical career. Sophomore Babbitt found these early goals "contemptible." Lacking a sense of purpose, he committed himself to "self-development in the widest sense." Like Columbus, he was sailing toward an unknown shore, yet was convinced "that my ship's head is pointed right."[22] And the right way was East.

Having taken so many courses that he needed only one more year to earn his degree, he took his junior year off and with an old high-school friend, A. P. Butterworth, sailed for Europe on a fifteen-

month poor-man's grand tour. Carrying their essentials in knap-
sacks, they slept in fields or cheap inns. Babbitt devoted himself
to meeting the people, absorbing the spirit of France, Spain, Italy,
and Germany, and learning new languages (he already knew Greek,
Latin, German, French, and the rudiments of Sanskrit). If the trip
did not provide a clear direction for his life, when he returned to
Harvard for his senior year the Ohio farm boy had at least become
more cosmopolitan.

This trip gave him time to sort things out. He could see America
through the eyes of other cultures and could begin to make some
sense out of his past reading. Crucial to the conversion he was
undergoing was his interest in the Orient and ancient Greece. These
cultures proved that the inner life could be more than delicate
fancies. As a sophomore, he sounded like his father in admiring the
"beautiful Buddhistic doctrine of a silent power that works to reform
the inert chaos of matter." But he also began to recognize Buddha's
"moral grandeur" and to admire India's saints for a will that carried
them unharmed through physical torment, even live burial. At first,
he may have simply been attracted to these things as an Oriental
equivalent to levitation and séances. Yet by the middle of his undergraduate career, Giese recalls, "unquestioned free will was the
most sacred tenet of his creed."[23]

He found other tenets in Plato and Aristotle. At the end of their
freshman year he and Giese read deeply in Plato's Socratic dialogues.
The Socratic method, Giese recalls, "gave Irving abundant handles
for discussion, especially for analyzing and exploding the arguments
for immortality." Among the arguments exploded were surely those
of Babbitt senior. Aristotle's *Nichomachean Ethics* taught Irving that
the end of man's striving is happiness, that happiness consists in
"good life and good action," and that good life and good action,
or virtue, "are destroyed by excess and defect" but "preserved by
the mean."[24]

One important influence was from the West—Matthew Arnold.
Significantly, however, Arnold called for an infusion of the Hellenistic spirit to balance the dominant Hebraic rationality of nineteenth-
century England. In *Culture and Anarchy* he argued that culture was
not an external display of manners and learning but the perfection
of the inner life, of what distinguishes human beings from animals.
Recognizing the age's one-sided devotion to everything mechanical
and external, Arnold saw a high standard for human striving in the

Greek ideal of "harmonious perfection" and "a human nature complete on all its sides."[25]

The call for internal working appealed to the introspective young Babbitt. He began to see that America did not need to escape into poetic reveries but rather to direct inward the expansive energy that produced its humming factories and bustling marketplaces. He would come to regret Arnold's emphasis on Hellenistic sweetness as opposed to Hebraic light because it encouraged aestheticism, and he would find inadequate Arnold's conception of religion as emotional morality. But his first scholarly article, "The Rational Study of the Classics" (1897), would echo Arnold in calling for "intellectual symmetry and sense of proportion" (*LC,* 154) and in defining culture as a demanding discipline that forms character. When he came to Harvard, Irving exhibited little symmetry; his dreamy inner life and vigorous outer life simply contradicted one another. By the time he graduated, his inner and outer lives were more of a piece—or at least he was convinced that they needed to be. Moreover, he believed that literary study, far from being an escape from the workaday world, could itself be one of the most serious kinds of work he could undertake.

In his senior year Edwin wrote that "you are getting old a little too fast. I don't want you to lose all your rollicking, playful disposition. It seems to me there is an expression that is not quite happy which is settling down over you." After all, modern life was becoming "more & more favorable toward angelhood."[26] But Irving was dedicated to earning his scholarly spurs, not a set of cherubic wings. He would rather strive for sainthood through moral effort in this world than frolic with the angels in the next.

Universal symbols and interesting fragments. When Babbitt graduated magna cum laude with honors in classics, he applied for a graduate scholarship, expressing a desire "to avoid the narrowness of specialism in retaining as far as might be its thoroughness."[27] He wanted to study modern languages and Sanskrit, but the graduate faculty probably thought he lacked a serious purpose and turned him down, though he had good reason to avoid the kind of specialized research graduate students were expected to undertake.

As chapter 5 will show, in the 1880s Harvard was in the middle of tremendous reforms instituted by President Charles William Eliot, who had emulated German universities dominated by *strengwissenschaftliche Methode* and *Lehrfreiheit*—rigorous scientific method ap-

plied freely in all areas of research. By 1891, Eliot would proclaim
that scientific method "characterizes the true university, and partly
justifies the name." Here was a comitatus united by a shared heroic
discipline practiced with almost religious zeal. As the renowned
psychologist G. Stanley Hall put it, "Wherever this real university
spirit of research breaks out, there is life; the Holy Ghost speaks
in modern accents; the old oracles find new voices, and who would
. . . not listen?"[28] Well, at least one Harvard student would not,
or if he did, did not like what he heard.

His senior year, Babbitt had taken Shakespeare from the new
English instructor George Lyman Kittredge. Babbitt sought to grasp
the moral significance of literature; Kittredge, of the new school of
philology, seemingly shared nothing of this concern. Lovers of words,
not ideas, philologists approached literature scientifically as a record
of historical language change. Babbitt had done well enough in
Greek under the philologist William Watson Goodwin, famous for
his *Syntax of the Moods and Tenses of the Greek Verb*. Kittredge he
could not abide.

In his yearlong Shakespeare course "Kitty" would go through
only five or six plays—almost line by line. Students left his course,
as one Harvard historian puts it, with "vast information" about
Elizabethan drama and life: "they had interesting fragments of such
a store of miscellaneous knowledge and wisdom as they had not
supposed until last year could be the possession of any one human
being."[29] But what did all these fragments signify? It would be
three years before Babbitt encountered a teacher who shared his new
belief in the high moral seriousness of literary study.

One of the last great Boston Brahmins, an intimate of Carlyle
and Ruskin, and one of America's first professors of art history,
Charles Eliot Norton was a thoroughgoing moralist. His son once
called his courses "Lectures on Modern Morals as Illustrated by the
Art of the Ancients." When Babbitt took Norton's Dante course
as a graduate student in 1892, he learned to judge literature by its
expression of universal moral laws. In his notes he recorded Norton
as saying that Dante "melted things in crucible of mind until dross
disappears—seeing permanent characteristics" and that "no man
recognized so thoroughly as Dante [in the *Inferno*] that acts of men
are not solitary[,] that every act is an effect and a cause—that sin
of whatever kind insists on its penalty and goodness insists on its
reward—universal value of symbolism."[30] This was heady stuff for

a young man raised on the moral pabulum dished up by Edwin Babbitt!

When Kittredge discussed a similar subject—the "eternal blazon" (or image of hell) King Hamlet's ghost finds too terrible for mortals to bear—he described, according to Babbitt's notes, only a curious linguistic construction in which the "Adj. takes function of first part of compound i.e. adj. and noun used together where we should expect two nouns with a prep." (that is, where we would expect "blazon of eternity").

Babbitt apparently refused to apply himself to the kind of work Kittredge demanded and, being naturally combative, may have had some run-ins with the man (a notorious classroom tyrant). Among all the As in Babbitt's academic record, one grade stands out; it is not even the "gentleman's C," but the slacker's C-. The embarrassment of such a judgment no doubt added to Babbitt's growing dislike of what he took to be the philologists' arrogant scientism. With their cursed Ph.D., philologists were squeezing out teachers who could lead a person to culture—in the Arnoldian sense. He detested them for it. And the feeling was mutual.

The Search for an Academic Discipline

At loose ends after graduation, Babbitt drifted back to Cincinnati and then on to New York, where his father was running something called The New York College of Magnetics. Owing money to his mother and perhaps his uncles, he took the first job offered through a teachers' agency. At the last minute, on 24 September, he received a telegram from the President of the College of Montana, a small Presbyterian school in Deer Lodge: "Will give board including rooms furnished lighted heated. Meats laundry and nine fifty answer my expense."[31]

The salary wasn't much, but he would at least be teaching Greek and Latin in a college—well, sort of a college. The school's three forlorn buildings overlooked a decaying mining town, whose sixteen saloons outnumbered its three churches. Furthermore, only 14 of the 130 students were in the traditional college curriculum; the rest were either in the Academy (taking college preparatory courses, typewriting, or stenography), in the conservatory, or in the school of mines. Babbitt spent most of his time teaching elementary Latin grammar and subjecting students to dreary daily recitations de-

signed, as the catalogue for 1889–90 put it, "to impart a valuable
mental discipline—to strengthen the memory, develop the reason-
ing faculty and reform slovenly and haphazard habits of thought."
This drudgery was not the kind of disciplined life he was looking
for. At the end of the spring semester of 1891 he headed East.

Two years of frugal living in Montana had given him enough
money to go to France, where he attended classes at the Collège de
France, the Sorbonne, and the Ecole des Hautes Etudes. He devoted
himself to gaining "a thorough literary and practical knowledge of
French, Spanish and in a lesser degree of Italian," rather than trying
to learn about "their historical development and philology."[32] At
the Ecole des Hautes Etudes he studied Sanskrit and Pali under the
Orientalist Sylvain Lévi and read independently in the early Buddhist
texts.

In France Babbitt found encouragement for his wide-ranging
study of literature, philosophy, and religion. *Religionswissenschaft*
(the history of religions) had emerged during the nineteenth century
as a new discipline, but there was no agreement on how it differed
from philosophy, theology, psychology, philology, or anthropology.
Most Europeans in the field found themselves attached to theological
faculties, except in France, where *Religionswissenschaft* was as respected as the sciences. Near the end of his year in Paris, Babbitt
wrote Harvard's Orientalist Charles R. Lanman that "My interest
in Sanskrit connects itself with Comparative Literature and Comparative Religion, rather than with Comparative Philology. While
I may not decide to make of it my specialty, properly speaking, I
shall in any case continue the study until I gain a considerable
familiarity with the classical Sanskrit on the one hand, and with
Pali and the Buddhist records on the other."[33]

In America "Comparative Religion" usually connoted the scientific classification of historical data and occupied the middle ground
between historical research into individual religions and the philosophy of religion, which generalized about the nature of religion.[34]
In using the terms Comparative Literature and Comparative Religion, Babbitt was perhaps hoping to make his studies acceptable
to the philologists. The tactic got him into Harvard's graduate
program at any rate.

However, he never did use a true scientific method, if by that is
meant a systematic induction from observed facts. His Harvard

graduate study suggested broad intellectual curiosity, not systematic investigation (he took courses in Sanskrit, Italian, French, German, and English). Despite his later claims to be a positivist, imaginative insight—not induction—underlay his mature creed. Although he would teach many of his courses in Harvard's Department of Comparative Literature, he did not share his colleagues' method. He was, if anything, striving to be a philosopher of religion, as well as of literature; that is, he was trying to formulate nontheological generalizations about the underlying unity of the religious experience. His approach was ethical and psychological and emerged from his readings in Buddhism.

Looking back on these years, Babbitt recalled that "I got in the old Buddhist books in particular the idea of dealing in a less dogmatic and more psychological way with certain problems of the inner life."[35] Of all the belief systems that contributed to his humanism, Buddhism was probably the most influential; some scholars have even concluded that he was actually a Buddhist, though he himself denied it. Babbitt favored Hinayana Buddhism, the so-called "Lesser Vehicle," as opposed to Mahayana, which transformed Buddha into a divinity and opened up salvation to all who lived a life of faith and compassion (and thus smacked of Edwin Babbitt's easy salvation). Buddha taught that all suffering comes from *dukkha* (thirst, or desire) and that the way to happiness and inner peace is through the elimination of desire. One could not grasp this truth through the reason; one had to put it into actual practice by following the "Middle Path" between hedonism and asceticism. However, if one willed ethical conduct and mental discipline, one would attain wisdom and eventually nirvana, a "blowing out" or "extinction" of thirst. Babbitt would not speculate about an afterlife, but he was attracted to the Buddhistic notion of karma, which asserted that every act has moral consequences determining the form a person's five "aggregates" take in the next life cycle. For him, the "essentially Buddhistic act is the rigorous tracing of moral cause and effect,"[36] the same kind of tracing Norton taught him to value in Dante. Like Buddha, Babbitt believed that the individual was solely responsible for his own spiritual life. "Self is the lord of self," he was fond of quoting from the *Dhammapada*. "Who else can be the lord?" And like Buddha, Babbitt based his humanism on what he insisted were observed facts of human psychology. Buddha's example gave his creed—and the literary study central to it—something like a scientific basis and made it, in his eyes, a discipline far more deserving of respect than philology.

Children of Light

That fall of 1892 Babbitt found himself one of two students in Lanman's advanced Sanskrit class. The other was a dreamy young poet from St. Louis, Paul Elmer More, who, unlike Babbitt, saw in Oriental religion a "pure spirituality . . . which has no attachment or relation to the phenomenal world or to concrete experience."[37] As an undergraduate, More had rejected his family's stern Presbyterian faith. He was now especially drawn to the mystical Sanskrit *Upanishads* and *Bhagavad Gita*.

These two men of opposite temperament forged a lifelong friendship during many long nights of heated argument. At age twenty-seven, after years of vigorous exercise, Irving had become an impressive man nearly six feet tall with a powerful, angular build, though he was already developing an arthritic stoop exaggerated by countless hours of slumping over books. More was struck most by his deep blue eyes, which usually had a distant, meditative look. In argument, Babbitt would gaze at the ground or over his opponent's shoulder, and then suddenly give a "swift direct glance that seemed to shoot out tentacles, as it were, into his very soul. At such moments that restless energy of Babbitt's, which was wont to work itself off in walking or by pacing back and forth as he talked, would appear to be gathered together, holding his body in an attitude of tense rigidity. The effect . . . was startling, sometimes almost terrific. . . ."[38] Under the assault, More yielded up his otherworldly beliefs and became Babbitt's most loyal ally in the war he would soon begin waging against modernism.

However, More's beliefs were not simply consumed in his friend's passionate arguments; his own enthusiasms fed Babbitt's intellectual fires. Working under Lanman, who was interested in the connections between Eastern and Western religions, More encountered F. C. Bauer's work on the Manichean heresy, *Das Manichäische Religions-system:* "Such mental excitement as that book gave me I had never known before and I have never felt since. It was as if the religious sense, like a drowning man, had laid hold of something solid to which it could cling. This was the principle of dualism. . . ."

More, the poet, found in the Manicheans' cosmic struggle between light and darkness a poetic vision of "the eternal problem of good and evil, of the thirst for happiness and the reality of suffering."[39]

The dual nature of man was hardly a new idea (Aristotle, Plato, Buddha, and Arnold all believed in it). But romanticism and evolutionism cooperated in identifying man with his instincts and conditioned habits. Babbitt seized on dualism as the touchstone for telling the true humanists—who recognized the opposition between the "law for man" and the "law for thing"—from the humanitarians—who asserted man's oneness with nature and who sought a utopia based either on sympathy or the conquest of nature.

Babbitt claimed this distinction as his one original contribution to humanism. (He never liked the label of *New* Humanism because he believed he was merely transmitting the wisdom of the past.) "Humanism," Babbitt felt, had become a debased term: "It is equally on the lips of the socialistic dreamer and the exponent of the latest philosophical fad" (*LC*, 3–4). He would spend many pages disentangling the term's historical meaning from modern corruptions.

The year 1892–93 was important for another friendship. Charles Eliot Norton, as we have seen, offered a salutary contrast to dry-as-dust philology. But he also validated Aristotle's notion that the good man is "the norm and measure" of all things. If Babbitt had any lingering faith in democracy, he soon adopted Norton's agnostic and aristocratic "true religion," the "utter absolute devotion" to "whatever men know and feel to be best." The next year More recalled three kinds of scholars at Harvard: the many business students, who cared only about big salaries; the less numerous *"verdammte dutch,"* who worked like mad in their specialties but never attained true Arnoldian culture; and the only two *"Children of Light,"* who "speak things worthy of Apollo" and whose light "is from within"—Charles Eliot Norton and Irving Babbitt.[40]

Babbitt's friend at Williams College that next year, Frank Mather, recalled that Norton was constantly on Irving's mind: "Charles Eliot Norton was actually living a life of strenuous moderation and sensitive decorum. It was the living presence of Norton that made the great sages of the past . . . come once more alive. . . ." A few years later, as an instructor at Harvard, Babbitt frequently visited Norton's Cambridge estate and submitted his early work for Norton's comment. He would eventually find Norton's aestheticism an inadequate counter to America's materialism and would see "the limitations of his mind on the philosophical side."[41] Nevertheless, Norton managed to combine strenuousness with his love of beauty, a balance Babbitt admired even though he himself inclined more toward strenuousness and an appreciation of the "spiritual athlete." Critics in the 1920s called humanism an abstract philosophy taken from books by ivory-tower academics. Babbitt knew better. Norton was a flesh-and-blood standard of decorum and moderation. And in Norton's unflinching stand against American imperialism in the Spanish-American War, a stand that brought vicious attacks from the jingoistic press, Babbitt found a model of grace under pressure that would serve him well. If a few such men could assume positions of leadership, they would, he believed, transform society. There is conviction in the preface to *Literature and the American College*, where he thanks Norton for encouragement, but above all "for an example." In the decorous but earnest conversations at Norton's Cambridge estate, perhaps Babbitt even found something of the camaraderie he had known around Wyoming campfires. Norton was an aristocrat to be sure, but his was a true aristocracy of virtue, open to anyone strong enough to practice its moral discipline.

Harvard and the Philological Syndicate

After taking his A.M. in 1893, Babbitt found a one-year job as instructor in Romance languages at Williams College, but the next year he was back on the job market. He wanted to return to Harvard and teach the classics but found no openings. However, in late May of 1894 President Eliot dismissed a French instructor caught plagiarizing.[42] The chairman of the French Department, Ferdinand Bôcher, needed to fill the vacancy quickly and recalled Babbitt as an A student in his French Composition class two years before. So by a twist of fate, Babbitt found himself teaching French at America's most prestigious university. This was a decision Bôcher would have cause to regret.

For four decades Babbitt remained an outsider in his own department but stayed even when he had lucrative offers elsewhere. One reason was Harvard's prestige. More important, perhaps, Babbitt needed opposition. With his dialectical habit of mind, he discovered truth largely by distinguishing it from error, and at Harvard he daily confronted what he perceived to be the errors of his age— in its educational policies, in his own colleagues, and in the very subject matter he was forced to teach. Unfortunately, he soon found those he attacked banded against him.

Babbitt barely survived his first few years on Harvard's faculty. The three senior men in the French Department—Bôcher, Philippe Belknap Marcou, and Frederick Caesar de Sumichrast—were all philologists who had little sympathy for Babbitt's kind of literary study. In addition, in his three courses at Harvard and one extra course at Radcliffe, he was teaching almost three hundred students in elementary French grammar and composition. It was Deer Lodge all over again, though instead of preparing students to read the classics he was becoming "a teaching automaton in order that Harvard sophomores may read French novels of the decadence in the original."[43]

To get out from under his crushing workload, he proposed advanced courses in the early Romantic movement and in French literary criticism. However, the "philological syndicate," as he began to call his colleagues, turned down his proposals. Worse yet, at the end of his third year they granted him only a one-year contract—"with the understanding that he may not be permanently retained, his work in the classes at present taught by him not being wholly satisfactory" (the "wholly" being inserted later as a mild qualification).[44]

The philologists had more than one reason to get rid of Babbitt. He had gone over Bôcher's head to Eliot seeking relief from the "wretched grind" of elementary courses. Moreover, he was quick "to deliver . . . crude and rash generalizations in conversation." Once, Giese recalls, he even told his chairman that French was "only a cheap and nasty substitute for Latin." Still, Babbitt felt victimized by a conspiracy. When More left his job at Bryn Mawr to write at an isolated old farm near Shelburne, New Hampshire, Babbitt wrote that "If I am thwarted here at Harvard much longer by such men as Sumichrast, I am likely to retire in disgust, too, and go out and cultivate some abandoned farm."[45]

Fortunately, in 1896 Radcliffe let him teach the advanced courses his own department had turned down. He did well enough there to impress the philologist Charles H. Grandgent, who helped get the Harvard French Department's approval for the criticism course. His future at Harvard was on the line, for in the fall of 1898, Sumichrast became chairman and refused to grant Babbitt more than a one-year contract, "it being understood that if he is successful in his new course, he will be recommended for such appointment next year."[46]

Because of Harvard's budget difficulties, Babbitt had to wait until 1900 to give the course there. The class, like all his others for several years to come, was small enough to meet around a table in the French library. When allowed to express his own ideas rather than drill students in grammar he was "lively and dramatic, . . . authoritative and magisterial, . . . 'Johnsonian.' " One of his earliest converts, Stuart Pratt Sherman, was often left befuddled by Babbitt's stream of apparently disconnected ideas, but he was nevertheless enraptured: "You felt that he was a Coleridge, a Carlyle, a Buddha, pouring out the full-stuffed cornucopia of the world's wisdom."[47]

President Eliot was not one to let a Coleridge or Buddha escape. In 1902, after eight years as a lowly instructor, Babbitt finally received his first promotion. At last he had in fact become Assistant Professor Babbitt.

However, not even a classroom Buddha could get tenure at Harvard without a string of impressive publications. (It took the popular teacher Charles Townsend Copeland eighteen years just to make assistant professor.) Babbitt had turned out a few articles on American higher education and on nineteenth-century French critics, as well as an occasional review, translation, and introduction to an edition. But his output was still small. He told More he was "holding back my ideas . . . until they are thoroughly mellowed by reflection." There was another reason—"caution." Although he believed he had a "certain cold judicial habit of mind," he confessed to a "vehemence of expression which comes in part from humorous exaggeration and partly from a mere impatience of the blood joined to my natural combative instincts in the face of contradiction."[48] The subject concerning him most was higher education, and what he had to say about it could only further alienate him.

But in 1908 Babbitt decided to go ahead. More and Norton shared his feelings about education and encouraged him to make them known, and Eliot's retirement that year made the timing seem right, even though Babbitt still worried about the philologists. This was a very critical moment for his career and his ideas. As later chapters will show in greater detail, *Literature and the American College,* which included several of his previously published essays, was not only the first full statement of the humanist creed but a devastating attack on trends in higher education. In the first three chapters, written especially for the collection, Babbitt carefully distinguished what he considered the true historical humanism from humanitarianism, the term he applied to philosophies claiming to be humanistic but failing to recognize a qualitative difference between life at the human and natural levels. In the remaining chapters he argued that the modern university with its humanitarian ideals was largely responsible for America's growing brutality and materialism. Whereas the old American college with its prescribed classical curriculum had educated all its students for wisdom and character and had produced a leadership class with shared ethical standards, the modern university with its proliferating courses and increasing emphasis on practical and scientifc studies was educating for service and power and producing leaders with no restraints on their lower impulses.

Because *Literature and the American College* ridiculed his own university's elective system and his colleagues' philological discipline, Babbitt knew he needed good reviews. More, by then literary editor of the prestigious *Nation,* had arranged a review by Paul Shorey, a classics professor at the University of Chicago. That was perhaps a mistake, for *Literature and the American College* satirized Chicago scholars for what Babbitt judged trivial research. The review, partly because of a *Nation* editor's cutting, gave the skimpiest idea of Babbitt's book and was "the kind of tepid stuff that will help a book on its way to oblivion."[49] In fact, the book sold so poorly that he had to borrow five hundred dollars from Giese to get his next one in print (not the first or last time the humanists would help each other out this way).

In 1910 he published *The New Laokoon,* which charged modern poets with confusing the genres, the same charge Lessing's *Laokoon* had made against the Romantics in the eighteenth century. However, the powers at Harvard were still not impressed, though the new president, A. Lawrence Lowell, read *Literature and the American College* with respect and appointed Babbitt to head the Honors in Literature Committee, giving him some chance to influence literature study at Harvard. Yet Lowell continued to offer Babbitt only short-term appointments and refused him a salary increase, even though Babbitt now had over eighty advanced students at Harvard and Radcliffe. The committee appointment was little consolation for years of being passed over in favor of much younger philologists. "I wonder," he fumed, "how long Harvard will continue its present policy of giving me first rate responsibility with second rate recognition."[50]

The showdown came in the spring of 1911, but now Babbitt had strong backing. His old student Stuart Sherman, then teaching English at the University of Illinois, got his dean interested in Babbitt. After visiting Illinois, Babbitt received an offer of a full professorship, the chairmanship of Romance Languages, and a salary of four thousand dollars (twice his Harvard salary). Not wanting to leave Harvard, he tried to use the offer to force Lowell's hand. It didn't work, though, and on 13 March the Corporation judged his promotion "unwise." Lowell concurred.[51]

At the last minute, however, two men backed his play. J. D. M. Ford, soon to be chairman of the French Department, wrote Lowell defending Babbitt as "one of the strongest and most successful teachers of Comparative Literature in the country" (high praise from a philologist). More also wrote protesting Lowell's shabby treatment of his friend (and perhaps insinuating some future unpleasantness in the editorial column of the *Nation*). Besides these big guns, More recalled, there was "the response to [Babbitt's] genius by a large and growing number of the better students."[52]

Under this pressure, Lowell backed down. On 20 March he wrote More that the Corporation's decision "does not mean that he will not be promoted [next year], but that we do not wish to decide the question in advance." More passed the letter on to Babbitt with the gleeful comment "I evidently scratched him a little." In February 1912 the Corporation voted Babbitt a full professorship and tenure. As late as January 1913, Illinois was asking Babbitt to name his own terms.[53] But by then he was determined to make a career at Harvard, for better or for worse.

He was forty-seven years old, and after eight years as instructor and ten as assistant professor he had technically won his way into the comitatus of scholars. Yet, as chapter 3 will show, he would find comradeship with men united in a common discipline only by forming a new comitatus, a "saving remnant" of academic men and journalists, mostly his ex-students, who would close ranks about the man they would call "General."

The Supremacy of Form

Babbitt had always found New England women "entirely too thin-blooded" for his taste, but in 1899 he had become attracted to a pretty, bright Radcliffe senior named Dora Drew, probably because she had grown up in the China Babbitt venerated, where her father was Commissioner of Imperial Customs at Tien-Tsing. The thirty-five-year-old French instructor and the twenty-three-year-old student fell in love, but in good nineteenth-century fashion Dora returned to China to think things over for a year. The summer of 1900, in a fitting mediation of East and West, Dora and Irving met in London and married.[54]

In Cambridge Irving rented a fashionable three-story home at 6 Kirkland Road, a small cul-de-sac a few minutes walk from Harvard Yard. He was determined his family would know more stability than he had; he lived in this house the rest of his life and raised his children there—Esther, born in 1901, and Edward, born in 1903. But he never overcame a sense of financial insecurity, for he never bought the Kirkland Road house or any other property even though extra courses at Radcliffe and lecture tours enabled him to provide Dora with a cook and housekeeper (at least until wartime and postwar inflation made that impossible). He also invested moderately in the stock market, sending Edward and Esther down to the mailbox each morning to fetch "Daddy's wallpapers" (the *Wall Street Journal*). He never really knew the kind of academic leisure he believed necessary for the humanist scholar, and felt at Harvard an "atmosphere of strain and high pressure" that led to his friend Josiah Royce's stroke in 1912 and to health problems of his own in 1915.[55] Although by making some shrewd deals he usually managed to get a bargain on a summer rental home in the resort of Dublin, New Hampshire, he spent these summers doing the writing he didn't have time for during the school year.

He eventually became a gracious host, but in the early years at least the obligatory academic dinners tended to be dreary affairs. When Dora began holding salons every Sunday during the academic year, Irving would usually retreat to his third-floor study. Only infrequently did he accompany Dora to the theater or the concert hall. He did, however, admire Mozart, who possessed "unsurpassed creativeness" while submitting fully "to the supremacy of form."[56]

The imposition of form on creative energy characterized Babbitt's own life. He impressed his friends with his tremendous vitality and yet had a moral conviction of the value of manners and decorum. In the summers, when the children were old enough, he instituted a family mixed doubles game played daily at the Dublin country club's tennis courts. He loved intense competition carried on within definite boundaries and by formal rules. For him, rules were one kind of convention, literally a "coming together" of human beings. The shared rituals of family and communal life supplied the greatest happiness he knew. The humanist who strives for proportion and decorum "will not indeed attain to any perfect communion," he wrote, "but he will be less solitary" (*R*, 348).

Although to be less solitary is no insignificant aim, at times Babbitt's decorum could become a barrier. As a young man, he had learned to distrust displays of emotions. Even his closest relationships were carried on within formal constraints. Dora did not presume an intimacy in her letters beyond a "Dearest I. B.," and More was never able to penetrate the "wall about his breast": "It is a little thing in that connexion, but significant, that for all our long and close friendship we never addressed each other except by our last names."[57] Moreover, his agnostic humanism was not entirely sufficient for the other Babbitts. Dora, raised a Unitarian, attended nondenominational services in Harvard's Appleton Chapel, Esther converted to Episcopalianism as a teenager, and Edward, drawn to the aesthetic side of the same religion, joined the choir of a Cambridge Episcopal Church.

But humanism imposed a form on Babbitt's own life and carried him through to the end. When his final illness came upon him in January 1932, he continued to work as before. Slowly ravaged by staphylococcus and streptococcus infections that produced a constant low-grade fever, weight loss, and skin eruptions, he continued lecturing until mid-April 1933, when he was forced to take to his bed. When Giese visited in late May, just a few weeks before his old friend's death, Babbitt was extremely weak but continued to read exams and theses. Giese was struck by "his stoicism and his courageous refusal to let circumstances dominate him" but begged him to rest. "When a man has been hired to do a job," Babbitt responded, "it's only decent to stick to it to the end."[58]

He finally died a miserable, indecent death, mumbling incoherently in a bed soaked with sweat. But his words to Giese recall an often-quoted passage from *Rousseau and Romanticism:*. "After all to be a good humanist is merely to be moderate and sensible and decent" (*R*, xx-xxi). It's easy to take this as a stultifying middle-class ethic or, as Edmund Wilson put it, "the unexamined prejudices of a Puritan heritage."[59] It wasn't though. To be decent is to be fitting and appropriate, and Babbitt tried to make his last days fitting and appropriate to the form of his life. His humanism was a prejudice—he would never deny that. But it was hardly unexamined. He dutifully submitted to what decades of reading and personal experience had convinced him was a higher law. As Emerson said in "Self-Reliance" of his own sense of personal duty, "If any one imagines that this law is lax, let him keep its commandment one day."[60]

Chapter Two
A Philosophy of Disciplined Choice

Perhaps the instability of his early life led Babbitt to seek in a centralizing philosophy the security he never found in his often-uprooted family. Perhaps his father's embarrassingly cheap and thoroughly American Spiritualism drove his intellect eastward to Europe and on to the Orient in pursuit of a deeper tradition. Perhaps his months in the American West gave him a thorough respect for the value of experience and action. But Babbitt's biography can explain the origins of his beliefs no better than the simple fact that he was an American who studied at an American college, immersed in American concerns. Even his apparent rejection of American literature—for he wrote little on American poetry and fiction that was not disparaging—is thoroughly American. Examples of Americans who needed a longer history, a deeper tradition, and a stricter sense of decorum extend from his self-exiled contemporary Henry James back to James Fenimore Cooper, and forward at least to Babbitt's student T. S. Eliot. In many ways Babbitt's philosophy is a continuation of an American tradition.

American Philosophical Roots

Jonathan Edwards.   Of Babbitt's American precursors the Puritan theologian Jonathan Edwards exerted the most significant influence on his thought. This claim may seem odd since he rejected vehemently Edwards's religion because of its "spiritual terrorism," "extremism," and "theological imperialism." Nevertheless, in Edwards's work, grace, "though associated with an impossible theology,"[1] functions much the same in its relationship to tradition as it does in Babbitt's philosophy.

Puritan theology asserted that God gave his Word (the Bible) to the children of Abraham (and the Puritans counted themselves among this number) so that they might live within a social order that could prepare them to receive grace and eventual regeneration. Reading the Bible on one's own was insufficient; if the Word were to prepare the unregenerate sinner to receive grace, it had to be received within the context of a society that had made a covenant with God. Those who had already received grace, the saints of the congregation, offered the sinner examples of the Bible's true meaning through their manner of speaking and acting. The problem, of course, was that the Bible, like any other text, was subject to multiple interpretation, as the dissension among the Protestants themselves forcefully demonstrated. The paradox here—that hearing the Word was necessary to receive grace, yet one's interpretation of the Word was suspect unless one had grace—is the focus of much of Edwards's writing.

Edwards's solution to the paradox was elegant.[2] He affirmed that man's purpose is to communicate with God and that all the communication from God man needed was contained in the Scripture. This communication, however, although it may be *known* by someone who has not received grace, cannot be *understood* except by someone who has. Therefore, grace cannot be a matter of new knowledge, a key to a puzzle. If this were the case, Scripture would be not only a necessary but also a sufficient preparation for receiving grace, since a saint could simply pass on the key to someone else, circumventing the need for God to directly convey His grace.

Edwards therefore described grace as a shift in perspectives. An unregenerate receiving grace is analogous to a barbarian suddenly receiving aesthetic taste: both can recognize a purpose and a unity that are not their own. As Edwards describes it, grace shifts one's perspective from that of finite self-love toward the infinite perspective of the love of "Being in general."

Babbitt does not describe grace as a shifting of perspectives, but he gives it a similar function. Grace provides a central purpose, a focus from which the entire tradition can be understood and evaluated. For Babbitt, this focus is the law of measure, a law that has been preserved throughout history through the agency of a "saving remnant" of humanists who recognize the tendency in man toward an excessive self-indulgence that can be curbed only if the individual adheres to standards that are not the product of his own longings.

Babbitt thought that Edwards's vision of life without grace was perverted. However, whereas Edwards "in his dealings with sin and

its reality is only exaggerating the facts . . ., Emerson and the
Rousseauists are simply repudiating the facts" (*M*, 358).

Ralph Waldo Emerson.   Babbitt both admired and detested
Emerson. He obviously felt that Emerson was worth reading—along
with Rousseau, Aristotle, Arnold, Goethe, and Sainte-Beuve, Emerson is mentioned frequently in Babbitt's published work. He often
cites Emerson's distinction between the "law for thing" and the
"law for man." He admires Emerson's concept of the "inner check"
and approves Emerson's view of the One and the Many. However,
in *The Masters of Modern French Criticism,* where Babbitt presents his
most sustained evaluation of Emerson, the review is mixed: Emerson
is "a somewhat baffling blend . . . of Rousseauism and insight"
(*M*, 361).

Emerson's "insight" was primarily his affirmation of an essential
human nature. When Babbitt mentions the ancient maxim that
"man is the measure of all things," he says that it can be interpreted
either sophistically or Socratically. As an example of a sophistic
interpretation, he quotes Anatole France: "All of us judge everything
by our own measure. How could we do otherwise, since to judge
is to compare, and we have only one measure, which is ourselves;
and this measure is constantly changing?" To this emphasis on man's
differences, Babbitt contrasts Emerson's intuition of sameness: "A
true man belongs to no other time and place, but is the centre of
things. Where he is, there is nature. He measures you and all men
and all events" (*M*, 345). According to Babbitt, Emerson attained
"a new sense of the unity of human nature—a unity founded, not
on tradition, but on insight" (*M*, 346).

Yet Emerson's very tendency to discount tradition disturbs Babbitt greatly. For example, in his essay "Quotation and Originality"
Emerson recognizes "how little the individual amounts to after all,
and how the best he can do is to quote and imitate." Nevertheless,
in the same essay Emerson adds, "to all that can be said of the
preponderance of the Past the simple word Genius is a sufficient
reply. . . . Genius believes its faintest presentiment against the
testimony of all history" (*M*, 350). Upon this Babbitt must ask,
"With such an inner oracle to rely on, why go through the severe
effort of building up standards based on the assimilation of tradition?" (*M*, 361).

Babbitt's hostility toward the doctrine of genius challenges Thomas
Nevin's conclusion that he was "a legatee, one of the last, of Amer-

ican transcendentalism."[3] In *Rousseau and Romanticism* Babbitt asserts that "The theory of genius is perhaps the chief inheritance of the New England transcendentalists from romanticism" and that its chief fault lies in its tendency to substitute the "discipline of technique" for the "discipline of culture" (*R*, 67). The theory encourages the individual, as Emerson says, to "plant himself indomitably upon his instincts" (*M*, 361), a singularly dangerous proposition given the instincts modern psychology has revealed in man. More dangerous, perhaps, is the tendency of "genius" to displace humility. If one trusts "in the private, self-supplied powers of the individual," as Emerson suggests, what restrains the idiosyncratic and eccentric desires that separate human beings and encourage pettiness and self love? "Emerson, then," Babbitt concludes, "is a wise man whose influence often works against that humility which is the first mark of wisdom" (*M*, 361).

William James.   If Emerson supplants Edwards's grace and tradition with genius as the guiding light for thought and action, Babbitt's contemporary William James retreats even further. In *The Will To Believe* James asserts that moral choice depends upon the peculiar temperament and passions of the individual: "Our passional natures not only lawfully may, but must, decide an option between propositions, whenever it is a genuine option that cannot by its nature be decided on intellectual grounds. . . ."[4] At least Emerson's genius transcends the peculiarities of the individual temperament and in some way connects one to the godhead, a Self shared by all. James, however, thinks that the individual's sensibility can be itself in tune with the morally ideal and that a belief in God can give the individual the courage to challenge the status quo.[5] Those with the most courage of this type, the saints, have escaped the constraints of society to such an extent that their "mystical" knowledge supersedes all logic and experience. James says it "is quite possible to conceive an imaginary society in which there should be no aggressiveness, but only sympathy and fairness."[6]

Babbitt considers the innate sympathy of James's saint to be a mere "simulation" of true religious vision: "True religious vision is a process of concentration, the result of the veto power upon the expansive desires of the ordinary self. The various naturalistic simulations of this vision are, on the contrary, expansive, the result of a more or less complete escape from the veto power, whether won with the aid of intoxicants or not" (*R*, 183). James's own association

of mystical experience with alcoholic intoxication is enough to damn
James's views on religion in Babbitt's eyes. In *Rousseau and Romanticism* Babbitt quotes at length from *The Varieties of Religious Experience:* ". . . alcohol . . . stimulate[s] the mystical faculties of
human nature, usually crushed to earth by the cold facts and dry
criticisms of the sober hour. Sobriety diminishes, discriminates and
says no; drunkenness expands, unites, and says yes. It is, in fact,
the great exciter of the *Yes* function in man" (*R,* 183–84). For
Babbitt, of course, such drunkenness could only accentuate the most
primitive of the individual's impulses. Men do not need assistance
to say Yes, they need it to say No.

Despite deep divisions between James's and Babbitt's thought,
they have much in common. Although Babbitt would consider
James's philosophy humanitarian rather than humanistic, many
commentators have in fact claimed that James was a humanist because, as Alburey Castell put it, he proposed "to deal with philosophies by referring them, in the last analysis, not to nature but to
human nature."[7]

In his *Pragmaticism as Humanism: The Philosophy of William James*
Patrick Kiaran Dooley expands on the same theme.[8] James, like
Babbitt, was concerned that philosophy had become too naturalistic,
too empirical, attending too closely to the physical side of man's
nature and not closely enough, if at all, to the spiritual or ethical
side. As Dooley points out, early in his career James chose to abandon
the theory of the "conscious automaton"—which claimed a complete
parallelism between mind and body—in favor of a theory of the
interaction between mind and body. James's dualistic, interactionist
view required the assumption of free will. On 30 April 1870 James
wrote in his diary, "My first act of free will shall be to believe in
free will."[9]

Again like Babbitt, James describes the process of free choice as
having both positive and negative moments. As Dooley summarizes:
"Each mental representation in the stream of consciousness automatically evokes a bodily response (consciously or unconsciously felt)
[the positive moment], and our freedom consists in our 'selective
attention' to mental representation A rather than the conflicting
representation B [the negative moment]. When we hold before our
mind, long enough, the representation A (instead of B) the self
(mind and body) responds with an appropriate action."[10] The dif-

ference between Babbitt and James on this point lies, first, in James's emphasizing the positive and Babbitt's the negative. A second differences lies in James's tendency to view the act of freedom as a purely internal struggle, emphasizing "the fact that volition is primarily a relation between, not our self and extramental matter, but between our self and our own states of mind."[11] Babbitt, however, will view the act as a struggle between internally generated impulses and an "outside" moral ideal.

At the question of where our moral ideals come from, James and Babbitt differ radically. In the last chapter of *Principles of Psychology* James compares the view of the evolutionists, who hold that the moral categories are simply the products of pleasurable and painful experiences, with those of the intuitionists, who hold that the categories are a priori and supersede all questions of utility. According to Dooley, James tries to combine the two. Society has the utilitarian task of weighing conflicting moral ideals in terms of the greatest good for the greatest number. As James says, "those ideals must be written highest which *prevail at least cost,* or by whose realization the least possible number of other ideals are destroyed."[12] However, in this act of balancing, society usually adjusts the ideal to fit the situation, rather than the reverse. In some cases, then, the moral man must go counter to his society: "The most characteristically and peculiarly moral judgments that a man is ever called on to make are in unprecedented cases and lonely emergencies, where no popular maxims can avail, and the hidden oracle alone can speak; and it speaks often in favor of conduct quite unusual, and suicidal as far as gaining popular approbation goes."[13]

Babbitt certainly would agree with the need to counter many of society's tendencies, but he would oppose James's "hidden oracle." For Babbitt, the proper authority to consult in the case of a peculiar injustice is not the inner self, but the normative values of a tradition, values imaginatively grasped by an individual to be sure, but values tested over time by civilization. Ironically, conformity to a tradition's most enduring values often means a radical nonconformity to the values of one's contemporaries.

Babbitt's life work, in the context of his American precursors, can be seen as a search for an adequate substitute for Edwards's divine grace, Emerson's genius, James's hidden oracle. This substitute Babbitt calls humanistic standards.

The Search for Standards

In his introduction to *On Being Creative and Other Essays* Babbitt announces his "attempt to solve the problem of standards" and to defend what he calls "a positive and critical humanism."[14] "Positive and critical" are the terms Babbitt uses again and again to describe his philosophic position. Despite the consistency of that position over a fairly long career, Babbitt never really adequately defines it, yet it controls his attitudes toward all the topics and issues that concerned him—in religion, politics, education, the arts, and especially literature. In this same introduction he says that the term "positive" indicates that he affirms a "higher will," while "critical" indicates the necessity of norms to check temperament intelligently. His philosophy is "humanistic" because he is not concerned with theological questions, only with the human question of "the bearing of this will on the mediatory virtues" (*O*, xxi).

The vagueness of these statements illustrates the difficulty of reading Babbitt for those accustomed to the more systematic critical theorists of the second half of the twentieth century. Babbitt was not systematic; he always considered his work to be tentative, exploratory, and even eclectic. As he says, "A philosopher who is not in this late age of the world highly eclectic may justly be viewed with suspicion" (*O*, xxxvi). His method, being highly Socratic, denied him the privilege of coining new terms and imposing new definitions. The truth of his topics lay buried in the folds and contours of discussion that had already taken place.

Beneath Babbitt's apparent vagueness, however, lies a consistent and important philosophical intention: "My endeavor has been to show that, even if one dispenses with absolutes, one may still retain standards" (*O*, xxii). He was not, however, searching for a particular set of standards; he was arguing for the necessity of having standards that are neither divinely revealed, nor arbitrarily imposed by society, nor merely determined by statistical norms.

For Babbitt, the proper source of human standards lies in human nature itself. His distinction between human and physical nature, which he describes most clearly in *The New Laokoon*, is central to his thought: "He [man] proves that he is set above nature, not so much by his power to act, as by his power to refrain from acting."[15] Natural, cultural, and psychological forces may compel the individual to act—to eat, to make love, to attend church—and although all creatures may be so compelled, only a human can refuse such compulsions, and a person is truly human only when refusing. As chapter 4 will detail, this belief in the necessity of refusal lies at the bottom of Babbitt's continual war with romanticism and naturalism, for both of these philosophies mock the individual's duty to refuse his own complusions. And for Babbitt, this is tantamount to denying man his humanity.

If one is human insofar as one can choose, the requirements of choice become the concern of humanistic philosophy. To choose, however, one must first distinguish. Meaning and significance are the products of distinguishing: a positive meaning always results from a careful exclusion of everything that it is not. And knowing what to exclude requires a standard.

Babbitt employs two fundamental kinds of standards he seldom confuses, but never explicitly distinguishes. First are the standards of conventional categorization, those standards which provide the individual with an interpretive link with others, present and past. Second are standards of purpose, which go beyond the conventional and make personhood possible. The difficulty of reading Babbitt arises partly from his tendency to use one term, "standards," to describe what are at least in practice different phenomena. For example, when criticizing the mechanical imitation of neoclassical art he says, "But though the truth cannot finally be formulated, men cannot dispense with formulae. The truth will always overflow his categories, yet he needs categories. He should therefore have formulae and categories, but hold them fluidly; in other words, he must have standards, but they must be flexible; he must have faith in law, but it must be a vital faith" (*NL,* 190). This statement, which seems vague, would have been clearer if Babbitt had said that conventional standards are subordinate to standards of purpose.

Conventional standards are for Babbitt the substrata upon which the higher reason does its work. At their lowest level conventional standards are simply the rules of a particular language: conventional syntax, diction, grammar, and so forth. At a higher level lies decorum, or manners; still higher are the "actual forms" of genre (discussed in chapter 4). These linguistic, rhetorical, and behavioral standards remain the individual's link to his culture. The individual who breaks them risks intelligibility and his moral bond with humanity. For example, Babbitt saw in the new surrealism an anti-traditionalism that "points to a one-sidedness in the movement from

the start, namely, to exalt the differences between man and man
and to disparage or deny the identities" (*O*, 126).

Babbitt's emphasis upon the importance of conventions provides
the essential background for understanding his famous distinction
between humanism and humanitarianism. Although it is true that
the humanist is "interested in the perfecting of the individual rather
than in schemes for the elevation of mankind as a whole" (*LC*, 8)
it is not true, as Thomas R. Nevin has claimed, that "Babbitt's
perspective is essentially Platonic." Like Plato, Babbitt assumed
that "the strengths and weaknesses of a society . . . are chiefly
those of the individual writ large."[16] But whereas Plato dreamed of
a society led by men having more or less direct access to the Truth,
it is precisely Babbitt's disgust with the social reformer's assumption
of his direct access to Truth that leads him to condemn humanitarianism. The humanitarian reformer's schemes for human perfection are formulae; formulae which perhaps approach the truth, but
formulae nevertheless which cannot be applied to society as a whole
without perversely distorting the experience of the individuals who
make up that society. In effect, the humanitarian reformer in the
most self-centered manner assumes the right to substitute his experience for and impose his values upon those he would reform,
denying their essential humanity.

The humanist's alternative to such reform is the self-reformation
of the individual. The humanist attempts only to persuade the
individual that his experience is limited and that his formulations
of the truth about the way things are and about the propriety of
his behavior should be tested against the experience of his fellows,
past and present. By accepting the conventions of the language and
his society as a norm, the individual simultaneously affirms the
value of others' experience and the fallibility of his own.

Obviously, then, the rules of ordinary decorum are as important
as the conventional linguistic and rhetorical rules. For Babbitt, the
customs and manners of society perform a necessary communi-
cative function. Yet he also believed that strict attention to conventional decorum for its own sake is just as dangerous to human
understanding as the most egregious impropriety. He fully supported Wordsworth's rejection of the artificial decorum of the upper
classes, but not without warning: ". . . there is a true as well as
an artificial decorum. Though the poet should eschew mere polite

prejudice, he cannot afford to neglect in his choice of words their conventional associations . . ."(*O,* 109).

Distinctions such as Babbitt's between "true" and "artificial" decorum would be subject to attack by relativist theories of linguistics, sociology, and aesthetics, especially after the publication of Saussure's theory of the arbitrariness of the sign. But Babbitt believed in an immediate perception "of something that abides in the midst of the phenomenal and transitory" (*O,* 142) in human behavior. True decorum was always bound up with "the constant factors in human nature" (*O,* 143) which provided an essential interpretive link between the individual and his culture as well as the cultures of the past. Babbitt thought it was possible, through an almost scientific process involving "the cooperation of imagination and analytical reason," for the artist and critic "to grasp these constant factors and in that sense attain to reality, even though this reality fall far short of being absolute" (*O,* 142–43). For the critic, this meant that it was possible to employ an almost universally applicable set of interpretive and critical standards, thus maintaining the crucial tie to the cultural past. For the artist, it meant it was possible "to build up a pattern of normal experience that one may imitate" (*O,* 143).

Babbitt's notion of "normal experience," however, should not be confused with average or typical experience. When defending Aristotle's doctrine of imitation in *The New Laokoon,* he carefully stresses Aristotle's insistence that the poet "should imitate things not as they are but as they ought to be" (*NL,* 9). The poet should offer us more than merely typical human action: "He should give us truth, but a selected truth, raised above all that is local and accidental, purged of all that is abnormal and eccentric, so as to be in the highest sense representative" (*NL,* 10). The Aristotelian doctrine of imitation, therefore, does not "fix [the poet] in a rut of convention and traditionalism" (*NL,* 9); rather, it gives the poet the liberty of higher, nobler standards that are capable of lending purpose and direction to human endeavors. Such standards of purpose are of a special origin. They are products of the "higher will."

The Higher Will

The conservative philosopher Claes E. Ryn has noted correctly that "To understand Babbitt, it is important to realize that in one sense will and imagination are the same."[17] Ryn gives the following example: "Even a seemingly simple impulse to quench one's thirst immediately translates itself into imagination. It becomes, for example, the intuition of clear, cool water passing down one's throat. Without articulating itself in concrete images, the desire to drink is unaware of itself, indefinite, and powerless to move the individual."[18] To Babbitt, any sort of action, whether Aristotle's symbolic action or the ethical action of everyday life, will necessarily have its imaginatively synthesized concrete object.

To understand Babbitt's views on the "higher will" and its relationship to the imagination, one must first grasp what for him was the simplest and most essential lesson of experience: in order to satisfy one desire one must necessarily refuse to satisfy any conflicting desires. One simply cannot get a drink of water and take a nap at the same time. Clearly, nature and culture provide the individual with an infinity of desirable objects, all vying for the will's attention, and clearly not all of them can be accommodated equally. Even simple survival requires that some desires be refused in favor of others more essential to existence. In this sense, the will—which Ryn defines as "the generic, categorized name for that infinity and variety of impulse that orients the individual to particular tasks"[19]— manifests both "higher and lower potentialities." Unfortunately, Ryn severely misinterprets Babbitt at this point and attributes to him his own rather typical moral view. He asserts for Babbitt a belief "that the human will is dualistic,"[20] that the will itself has higher and lower drives, and that satisfying the one will lead to a spiritual existence while satisfying the other will lead to a hedonistic one.

Nothing could be further from Babbitt's view. For Babbitt, the *objects* of desire, not desires themselves, exhibit a dualistic character, and they attain this character only in terms of whether they contribute toward or detract from one's overall aim. Babbitt is not concerned that following one's immediate impulses will lead to a life of pleasure; he is concerned that it will not. But for him pleasure and happiness are possible only if one chooses the objects of one's desires. If one accepts the objects one's immediate situation offers, then one's life is essentially driven, without freedom. True freedom lies in the pursuit of a chosen goal. This means that lesser objects more immediately attainable have to be denied. But there are no lower, satanic drives that need to be repressed, and there are no higher, angelic ones that if given their heads will pull the self toward salvation.

Babbitt's philosophy is best conceived as one that provides the individual with a way to resist being determined by environmental, cultural, and psychological forces. To combat these forces and escape such determination, Babbitt suggests, the individual must choose a goal or purpose comprehensive enough to require the complete attention of one's faculties.

On this point T. S. Eliot expressed his deepest apprehensions about Babbitt's humanism. In Eliot's view, only religion can provide such a comprehensive goal or purpose. Humanism, Eliot contends, does provide a necessary check to extreme tendencies, but it does not, cannot, supply a substitute for religious vision. "What," he asks, "is the higher will to *will,* if there is nothing either 'anterior, exterior, or superior' to the individual?"[21] In Eliot's eyes, Babbitt's humanism is too positive, promoting a particular way of life as a substitute for religion when it should confine itself to its negative function. Humanism is "essentially critical—I would even say parasitical"[22] since it cannot through its own agency provide the purpose for life on which its own functions depend.

Eliot's complaint is partially justified. Babbitt himself seems either confused or else, for rhetorical reasons, intentionally vague on this point. He will go no farther than to accept the necessity of grace. He certainly does not promote any particular religious vision, yet he certainly does hold up the visions of Christ, Buddha, and Confucius as examples of the sort of thing he does promote. The problem here, however, is one of point of view. As a Christian, Eliot believes that the Christian vision is true, true for all times and all places. But Eliot accepted not only the vision but also the metaphysics, the dogma, the ritual, and the other trappings of conventional religion whose significance dies with the historical situations that produced them. For Babbitt, the core of the vision might endure, but not the rest. Eliot's speculation that Babbitt "knows too many religions and philosophies, has assimilated their spirit too thoroughly . . . to be able to give himself to any"[23] comes very close to explaining why Babbitt would not, as a humanist, commit himself to any particular religious vision.

Although Babbitt refused to declare that an adequate vision could have only a divine source, he did believe that one should pursue some vision of a purpose for human life. However, the purpose must be one that represents, in the situation at hand, a balancing of opposing forces: it must conform to what Babbitt calls the "law of measure." The law of measure is Babbitt's "highest law": it supersedes all other laws, and it takes precedence over all desires, whether those generated by the body or by a religious vision. Contrary to Ryn's belief, Babbitt does not deny the significance of any human desires. He recognizes, however, that desires tend toward extremes, and such tendencies deny the significance of their opposites. For example, the desire to express one's peculiar feelings tends to lead to a denial of communal feelings. Thus, typically one's desires will tend toward extremes and will not represent the full range of human potential.

Babbitt believed that the ability to distinguish the truly representative from the merely typical was a gift. The term he used to describe this gift, "grace," suggests that his humanism was a thinly disguised theology. However, Babbitt informs his readers that the Christian concept of grace is in fact derived from the earlier Greek notion of grace as a supernatural guide for reason.

Such a guide is essential. It is important to remember, however, that for Babbitt such guides are never merely abstract philosophical propositions; they must be made concrete, capable of being grasped by the imagination and put to practice in particular situations. This necessity explains why he values literature so and why he most admires those "philosophers" whose lives illustrate their teachings. Babbitt often presents the life of Christ as an example of grace at work, but as Ryn points out, "Jesus of Nazareth does not present man with a new philosophy, to be tested on abstract philosophical grounds. Jesus asks men to follow him, that is, to perform Christ-like actions."[24] Only an illustration of a doctrine at work within a specific situation can demonstrate that doctrine's capacity to mediate extremes, to preserve the past and project the future within the tension of the present. Christ's actions, for example, were always counter to the prevailing tendencies of his day, but at the same time his actions did not negate the beliefs and customs of his time. He threw the money changers out of the temple; he did not burn down the temple. Grace does not revolutionize thought; it does not abandon tradition: it fulfills it by allowing one to recognize a model that will restore the significance of whatever desires the extremism of the moment has diminished.

Thus grace provides the example, the imaginatively grasped symbol of purpose, which reason can then follow. Grace is superrational and supernatural only in the sense that the model it provides cannot be derived logically from the present state of affairs. Despite the theological terminology, and despite Babbitt's refusal to deny that grace may be a divine gift, as far as his philosophy is concerned where the gift comes from is irrelevant. The man tests the gift; the gift does not test the man. One cannot know in advance whether the cross or the swastika is a proper symbol for a goal of human endeavor. As products of the imagination, such symbols are non-rational. They therefore must be tested by reason and by experience. If pursuing the goals such a symbol represents does more to increase than to diminish the spirit, we may be inclined to believe the gift is divine, since there can be no rational explanation for why one should work and another should not.

Humankind, for Babbitt, bound in all directions by three immense sets of laws—those of physical nature, of reason, and of a tradition—finds that the freedom to choose, truly to choose, is very rare indeed. Of course, one may act unnaturally, unreasonably, or inhumanly, yet such illegitimate choices will lead certainly to suffering or destruction. Thus the choice to desire something that does not deny natural, reasonable, and human desires but that nevertheless is not merely a desire produced by felt impulses is rare—a gift. One cannot claim credit for such a desire, for the individual's capacity to think and act and, more important, to will are bound up inextricably with the categories that govern his perception. This is why, for example, Babbitt criticizes Julien Benda's attack on Bergson, whose position Babbitt assuredly detested. Benda's weakness was his "failure to recognize that the opposite of the subrational is not merely the rational but the superrational, and that this superrational and transcendent element in man is a certain quality of will" (*O,* 199).

This, then, is Babbitt's "higher will," the positive side of his humanism, a will "associated traditionally with the operations of God's will in the form of grace"[25] but now secularized to indicate any desire that is free from the categories that govern impulsive human actions. The higher will will seek an object that conforms to the "highest law"—"the highest law as a law of concentration,— a law of unity, measure, purpose" (*NL,* 202). What grace gives, in other words, is a purpose that, if pursued with disciplined diligence, brings order out of chaos, the one out of the many, significance out of meaninglessness. "To have standards," Babbitt says in "What I Believe," "means practically to have some principle of unity with which to measure mere manifoldness and change" (SC, 242). This statement summarizes the positive side of his philosophy. His teleological view insists that a poem, a political state, or a man's life must be organized about some single, encompassing desire to which all others are subordinated if that poem, state, or life is to achieve any sort of significance.

The higher will must accomplish this aim through the power of imagination: "There is a power in man, often termed imagination, that reaches out and seizes likenesses and analogies and so tends to establish unity" (SC, 242). One can will to achieve only those objects of desire that the imagination has synthesized from the flux. The imagination, however, is itself indiscriminate. It can and most assuredly will produce objects of desire that cannot be integrated with a total vision: one may have an urge to scratch one's buttocks even as one addresses the multitude. Thus the imagination must be subordinated to the *higher* will if it is to create anything of significance. Incomplete or partial aims may produce formally complete poems or powerful lives; still, the poem may be trivial or the life may be mad or destructive. Accordingly, the higher will—the will to achieve the complete vision—must for the most part exercise its censure. It must negate those impulses that would interfere with its highest aim. (Here one should note that such negated impulses are not in themselves "evil" or even "lower," except insofar as they do not contribute to the higher aim. To say they were would be analogous to saying that the marble that must be chipped in order to sculpt the statue is of a lower order than the marble that remains.)

Just as important as the positive aspect of humanism, therefore, is the negative or critical aspect. Unfortunately, too many of Babbitt's critics have overlooked the positive and thus have balked at the negative. Allen Tate, for example, has asserted that for Babbitt "The good man is he who 'refrains from doing' what the 'lower nature dictates,' and he need do nothing positive."[26] Similarly, Henry Hazlitt claims that Babbitt's focus "is always on the purely *negative* virtues."[27] Some critics have gone so far as to assert that Babbitt's personality was incapable of any sort of affirmation.[28] Babbitt knew that his ideas might elicit such responses: "The paradox of the whole matter is this: the philosophy of the 'inner check' when put theoretically and in terms of the intellect seems intolerably negative. But when this philosophy is actually *lived*, when it becomes incarnate in a personality the inner check is thus felt, not as something negative, but as a positive driving power. This is only another way of saying that the key to life is found not in the intellect but in the will."[29]

But the key to the will is found in the imagination. Babbitt recognized that the term *imagination* historically has been "used primarily to describe the various impressions of sense or else a faculty that was supposed to store up these impressions" (*O*, 102). For Babbitt the synthetic power of the imagination can act only on those impressions that have become separated from actual experience. The imagination "therefore gives only appearances and not reality" (*O*, 102). Whereas only the imagination can derive order from the chaotic flux of experience, the imagination alone cannot guarantee the validity of the unity it presents. "The unity thus apprehended," accordingly, "needs to be tested from the point of view of reality by the analytical intellect—the power that discriminates—working not abstractly but on the actual data of experience" (*SC*, 242).

What Babbitt means by "the actual data of experience" differs considerably from what the positivists of his time meant by it. As Ryn has noted, Babbitt believes that scientists in general "are not really attentive to the full range of human experience but arbitrarily select fragments of it or distort it through methodological reductionism."[30] A true positivism cannot be satisfied merely with an "accumulation of 'data' in the empirical sense": it will attempt to acquire "a firmer grasp of the oneness or unity of life that abides in the midst of change and diversity."[31] This means that all propositions about human nature, whether "scientific" or "fictional," need to be weighed against similar propositions of the past in order to gauge the wholeness of their vision, and they must be tested and evaluated in terms of how they will affect the life of the individual who accepts them as truth.

Babbitt's famous "inner check" therefore functions in two ways. First it constrains the imaginatively grasped unity of purpose by weighing it against experience, experience conceived broadly to include both that of the individual and that of his tradition. Second, it constrains the individual's own impulses, those which would move her to act against her own chosen purpose. As Ryn has put it, "In its relation to what is destructive of our spiritual unity, the higher will is felt as a restraint. The moral end is advanced by censuring what is opposed to it."[37]

If Babbitt doubts "the value of the imagination that is thus free to 'wander wild,' that is not in other words disciplined to any norm" (O, 91), he equally doubts the value of imaginationless truth. In literature especially, truth and fiction must cooperate. Truth alone is bloodless, without any vital purpose. For this reason, in "The Problem of the Imagination: Dr. Johnson," Babbitt criticizes the great neoclassicist's otherwise commendable attention to decorum; for when Johnson discusses the relationship between truth and fiction, he "inclines to set the two in sharp opposition" (O, 84). If Johnson had done justice to the role of fiction or illusion in both life and art, the romantics would have had nothing to rebel against: "As it was, these rebels simply took over the neo-classic opposition between reason and imagination and turned it upside down" (O, 93).

The Need for Dualism

This last statement is typical of how Babbitt describes transitions between movements in human history. Values tend to shift from one extreme to the other—from too much discipline to too much freedom, from formalism to expressionism, from synthesis to analysis. But the humanist's goal—"poised and proportionate living" according to "the law of measure" (SC, 229–30)—cannot be achieved within any sort of hegemonic system. True humanism must be both positive and critical. A man should pursue the realization of some goal, yet "a man must humanize his gift" (O, 127–28), discipline it to the known laws of nature and humanity. Such humanization is impossible, however, unless the goal somehow transcends the boundaries of conventional categorization. If it does not, then the critical side of philosophy becomes merely negative and destructive. Since human thought is by nature categorical, the promotion of one pole of a categorical opposition will require the negation of another. For Babbitt, though, true thought will always recognize the force of both elements.

Thought that does not recognize both elements of a dialectical opposition will ultimately end in perverse monism. "Monism," Babbitt says in The New Laokoon, "is merely a fine name that man has invented for his own indolence and one-sidedness and unwillingness to mediate between the diverse and conflicting aspects of reality" (*NL,* 226). Becoming "novel" is easy for the monist—all he has to do is take over the categories of his predecessors and promote the opposite side. Thus the history of human thought is too often a record of movement from one form of critical indolence to another: "For the neo-classical indolence of mechanical imitation the romanticist substituted the indolence of revery—of a spontaneity that has only to let itself go" (*NL,* 188). Submission to the logic of form is as lazy as submission to one's own appetites. Any form of extremism, every monistic belief falls short of the "rounded view" of humanism.

Humanism, accordingly, must assert a thoroughgoing dualism. If the modern world is to save itself, Babbitt believed, it was "imperative to re-establish the true dualism" (*SC,* 241). In the context of this last quotation, false dualism is the humanitarian opposition between the individual and society that solidifies even as it denounces destructive distinctions. The chief exemplar of humanitarianism (and for Babbitt of almost every other foolish idea at work in the modern world) is Rousseau. Humanitarianism is the product of the "sudden vision" that came to Rousseau on his famous walk from Paris to Vincennes in 1749, a vision which taught him, among other things, that "man is naturally good and that it is by our institutions alone that men become wicked" (Rousseau, in *SC,* 227). According to Babbitt, Rousseau's false new dualism between the naturally good man and his institutions has displaced the older, Christian dualism between good and evil in the heart of the individual. Although to Babbitt the facts of history completely discredit the theory of natural goodness, proving that "the will to power is, on the whole, more than a match for the will to service" (*SC,* 232), even more damning than the facts are the consequences of adhering to the theory, for the theory shifts the burden of responsibility from the individual conscience to the collective conscience of society. Babbitt gives as an example Rousseau's excuse for abandoning his five children, that "he had been robbed by the rich of the wherewithal to feed them" (*SC,* 239). Rousseau's act, says Babbitt, is merely "an evasion of moral responsibility" seemingly justified by Rousseau's humanitarian philosophy, but in reality only an indication of "a naive willingness to shift the blame onto something or somebody else" (*SC,* 240).

But Rousseau and the "modernists" are not the only evaders of moral responsibility. Equally irresponsible are the traditionally religious, most especially the Roman Catholic who "has in matters religious simply repudiated individualism" (*SC,* 233), and the scientist who allows the disinterested attitude of method to replace his own will and who disclaims responsibility for the uses to which his discoveries are put. The scientist's attitude is the more outrageous simply because it is the more dangerous: "If Professor Compton or another succeeds in releasing the stores of energy that are supposed to be locked up in the atom, we may be sure that he will feel immaculate, whatever the practical consequences of his discovery, even though men use it to blow themselves off the planet; for he is a servant of *pure* science" (*O,* 174). Although Catholicism and science may be commendable to the extent that they are disciplinary, they are nevertheless exercises in discipline that eschew the individual's access to the higher will and therefore are ultimately destructive to the human spirit.

The higher will generates man's ability to transcend his given categories and thus control his instincts by establishing the true dualism, an opposition between élan vital and *frein vital,* which Babbitt translates as vital impulse and vital control (*SC,* 235). In Babbitt's work this is the most general opposition from which all others he writes about—form and expression, synthesis and analysis, expansion and concentration—derive. The higher will asserts both vital impulse and vital control. Babbitt takes it as a methodological given that "any point of view works out into an ironical contradiction of its own principle, unless it is humanized through being tempered by its opposite" (*LC,* 43).

Accordingly, he refuses to establish a hierarchical relationship that can be inverted and therefore "deconstructed" and forced to assert its opposite. Humanism does not allow one side of an opposition to overcome or replace the other: "Expression can never become form or form expression any more than expansion can become concentration or the centrifugal the centripetal. But though form and expression can never be actually merged, it is plain from all that has been said that they should stand toward one another not as clashing antinomies but as reconciled opposites" (*NL,* 230–31). True human being depends on the freedom of measure, the capacity to choose, for example, what of expression or what of form is necessary to accomplish a certain purpose in a given situation. To have less than that capacity is to become a slave to the logic of one's own categories. The higher will guarantees that capacity. Therefore, if the higher will holds, man's access to spiritual freedom is assured. Accordingly, the humanist must "affirm it first of all as a psychological fact, one of the immediate data of consciousness, a perception so primordial that, compared with it, the denial of man's moral freedom by the determinist is only a metaphysical dream" (*SC,* 234–35).

Because of their failure to affirm the higher will, monistic philosophies encourage not only indolence and moral irresponsibility, but also aimlessness. Babbitt takes up this point most commonly with regard to aesthetics. Benedetto Croce, for example, reduces all art to expression, but in so doing he deprives art of the ability to express anything. By recognizing only the artist's intuitions of sense, Croce "sneers" at the higher intuitions that alone can give art a humane purpose. Without a central vision, a principle of selection with which to organize the impressions of sense, the expressive aspect of art becomes as irrelevant to man's needs as conventional formality. In either case, art cannot say anything significant, and for Babbitt "true art consists in having something to say and then saying it simply" (*NL,* 230).

Antinomial philosophies, such as Kant's, also deprive art of the ability to make a significant point. Although Kant affirms a higher will grounded in the supersensible, he denies that man has access to that realm. Needless to say, the "sharp divorce that Kant establishes between the noumenal and phenomenal involves him in extraordinary difficulties, especially in dealing with the idea of freedom" (*O,* 143–44). The chief difficulty lies in its forcing Kant to "proclaim that genius and imitation are incompatible" (*O,* 147). He could emancipate the imaginative genius and yet restrain it from aimlessness only by showing "by dint of metaphysical subtleties that art may have a purpose which is at the same time not a purpose" (*O,* 147). For Babbitt, this means that Kant's play of the imagination can be only an irresponsible play, since the categorical imperative's abstractness leaves the artist with little more than his own sentiment to provide him with a purpose. Thus it was easy for Schiller, when he took over Kant's play theory, simply to eliminate purpose from it entirely.[33]

The deficiencies of monistic and antinomial philosophies confirm Babbitt's belief in the necessity of a dualism that affirms both sides of any logical opposition, measuring the relative need to promote one or the other in any given situation, but never claiming one absolutely and for all time. For Babbitt, then, the true and false of categorical logic are not applicable to human issues: "We are not to suppose that because a man has made some progress in mediating between opposite virtues and half-truths he has therefore arrived at the truth. The Truth (with a capital T) is of necessity infinite and so is not for any poor finite creature like man. The most any man can do is tend toward the truth . . ." (*NL*, 189). Replacing truth and falsity with the more human choice between propriety and impropriety, Babbitt's humanism can never become a dogmatic set of beliefs that justify extremism—any form of domination. Humanism is not a canon of truths; it is a way of being in the world.

For Babbitt, being in the world means being in the present. The standards that form one's desires must be adjusted for the present situation, for the here and now. Babbitt's chief criticism of all forms of romanticism—in *Rousseau and Romanticism* he attacks writers as diverse as Schiller, Holderlein, Poe, Ruskin, and Hegel—is that the forms of romantic desire never lie within the possibilities of the present, but in the distant past, in the distant future, even in infinity. The romantic's "primary demand on life is for some haven of refuge; . . . he longs to be away from the here and now and their positive demands on his character and will" (*R*, 90). The extreme forms of monistic and antinomistic desire lie beyond any possible realization and thus relieve the romantic of agonizing deliberation and choice.

Humanistic Method

Babbitt once wrote to Paul More: "It is my conviction that if the critic is to exercise a useful function he cannot afford to get too much out of touch with the contemporary situation."[34] What Babbitt calls "humanistic method" differs from the "disinterested" method commonly associated with the sciences precisely because it takes into account the changing situation of its practitioners. As Babbitt tirelessly repeats, physical nature is essentially different from human nature because human beings can refrain. That ability guarantees choice in terms of a purpose, so that humanistic method must always be not only a "critical" method but also an "interested" method—its practitioners seek not only to distinguish but also to establish standards. Thus the method must always take into account that the goals of thought (should) exceed the concepts with which the thought is accomplished. The present cannot be grasped entirely with the terms of the past.

Humanism demands, therefore, that the sensibility of its practitioners should not be forced to accommodate its method, but that its method should be capable of accommodating the sensibility of its practitioners. When method becomes overly rigid, it allows the critic to observe only those patterns the method itself has imposed. The result is that the critic loses his ability to deliberate upon the appropriateness of his use of the method. In short, he loses the capacity of choice.

Of course, as we can observe from Babbitt's severe criticism of almost every major movement in Western philosophy, men do tend to reduce their own capacities for choice and slip into the grips of monism: "If the philosopher does win a glimpse of something beyond the almost impenetrable veil of illusion, he is liable to take for the truth what is at best only a half-truth, and so grows one-sided and fanatical. The half-truth often gets itself formulated and imposed tyrannically upon the world, and men continue to hold fast to it long after it has served its purpose, when emphasis is needed rather on some opposite aspect of the truth" (*NL,* 187). Humanism recognizes that a "truth" or a principle of action is useful only insofar as the situation for which it was formulated remains, and that a situation itself is defined by a sometimes noble but always thoroughly human purpose of an individual though it be defined in terms of the general categories of logic and language. "The essence of any true humanistic method," therefore, "is the mediation between extremes, a mediation that demands of course not only effective thinking but effective self-discipline" (*NL,* 189).

The first step of humanistic method is to establish the right attitude toward conventions. Humanistic method has two primary aims—establishing standards and examining conventions—and both converge upon the chief goal of humanism, extending the possibilty of human happiness. For Babbitt, standards and conventions are the same phenomena looked at from different perspectives: conventions are established standards; standards establish new conventions. However, humanistic philosophy never flouts established beliefs and customs simply for the sake of it.

This flouting of convention (which, as one might expect, Babbitt terms "Rousseauistic") is characteristic of romanticism in general. It is a sort of disdainful distancing from a present state of affairs, one Babbitt usually describes as "romantic irony," whose theory was first worked out by Friedrich Schlegel and then taken up by Schiller, Fichte, and Novalis: "When a man has taken possession of his transcendental ego . . . he looks down on his ordinary ego and stands aloof from it. His ordinary ego may achieve poetry but his transcendental ego must achieve the poetry of poetry. But there is in him something that may stand aloof even from this aloofness and so on indefinitely" (R, 241). Such an attitude toward convention, toward "what his age holds to be normal and central" (R, 242), will always involve the philosopher in paradox, for "the man who is moving away from some centre will always seem paradoxical to the man who remains at it" (R, 246). However, Babbitt insists that there are two directions from which one may move from a center, from conventional normalcy.

Romantic paradox is centrifugal, moving away from whatever is at present considered central, to the extent that the romanticist "inclines to measure his own distinction by his remoteness from any possible centre" (R, 242). Classical paradox, however, is centripetal, and the classicist tends to move from an older, established center toward a new center that is considered even more central. Both the romantic and the classical attitudes toward convention are ironic. Neither takes conventions at face value. But the ironic contrast in romantic writing is usually between a stale, rigid didacticism, which the romanticist takes to be a false absolute, and an expansive, relativistic freedom of the ego; whereas the ironic contrast in classical writing is usually between an older, partially true axiom of common sense and a newer insight more representative of human nature and thus truer.

The chief advantage of the classical over the romantic in this case is that while the romantic attitude pushes toward the eccentric, usually in the form of a longing for infinity, the classical attitude pulls toward the concentric, usually in the form of a more definite end upon which the individual can concentrate his efforts. The most significant classical ironist, Socrates, contrasts what men take to be knowledge with "true and perfect" knowledge, a knowledge finite man cannot attain, but one toward which he can aim. To the dogmatist, "the man who thinks he has achieved some fixed and final centre" (R, 244), Socrates seems to be a skeptic. Babbitt agrees that Socrates' attitude "implies a certain degree of detachment from the received beliefs and conventions of his time" (R, 244), yet

Socrates never becomes completely detached nor does he mock convention simply because it is convention: "While working out the new basis for conduct he continues to observe the existing laws and customs; or if he gets away from the traditional discipline it is towards a stricter discipline; if he repudiates in aught the common sense of his day, it is in favor of a commoner sense" (*R*, 245). The main difference between romantic and classical irony is that "What the romantic opposes to convention is his 'genius,' that is his unique and private self. What Socrates opposes to convention is his universal and ethical self" (*R*, 245).

A typical error of the classicist occurs, however, once he believes that he has in fact achieved that universal self. This will lead, as it did occasionally for Socrates, to becoming "needlessly unconventional and also unduly inclined to paradox" (*R*, 245). The ironic attitude of true humanism must always include an element of humility: A certain knowledge that one's own high standard may in another set of circumstances be no more than another convention involves a corresponding knowledge that today's conventions are likely to contain within them an element of truth that cannot be lightly discarded.

The humanist considers it his duty to retrieve that truth; he therefore concentrates his first efforts upon examining those central, conventional formulations of the concepts that guide human endeavor. Such concepts cannot be evaluated, however, until the general terms that designate them have been analyzed. For a teleological philosophy such as humanism, general terms must have clearly understood meanings, for the ends that give life meaning become fully concrete only in language (since the ends are ideal and finite man can never attain them). It is therefore necessary to preserve the historical meaning of general terms—to examine them as they have actually been used, retrieving the central, motivating factor from the various ancillary meanings that always accrue to words. The alternative is to define a term arbitrarily, like a mathematician, then to compare that definition to past definitions. The trouble with such an approach is that one will be inclined "to take as primary in a more or less closely allied group of facts what is actually secondary—for example, to fix upon the return to the Middle Ages as the central fact in romanticism, whereas this return is only symptomatic . . ." (*R*, 2–3).

Babbitt's method is therefore historical, but it is not the "historical method" common to his time. His unusual understanding of history has led some of his critics to assert that he denies the relevance of history to literature. For example, Thomas R. Nevin says that Babbitt's "stylistic bias necessarily neglected any correlation between historical and literary developments, such as the rise of an industrial bourgeoisie from the First to the Third French Republic and the rise of the novel."[35] Nevin comes closer to an accurate assessment of Babbitt's view when he says that "To explain literature through history was," Babbitt felt, "a perverse inversion of method: history was to be understood through literature just as, according to Aristotle, particulars were illumined by universals."[36]

Like most of Babbitt's critics, Nevin fails to recognize that Babbitt does not distinguish sharply between "literature" and "nonliterature," between factual and fictional texts, as will the formalist theorists who follow him. As chapter 4 will explain more fully, Babbitt recognizes an essential difference between local generic differences and generic differences proper, the latter representing the universal standards against which local changes are to be measured.

Since these standards represent a balancing of extreme views, not a fixed opinion which remains the same for every situation, structuralistic critics who depend upon a fixed point of view often see in Babbitt's thinking either purposeless vacillation or an even more deadly historical sin—relativism. Nevin, for example, calls attention to Babbitt's note on Blaise Pascal that comments on "Pascal's comparison of the person of faith with someone who has a watch among others who have none": "Unfortunately," Babbitt rejoins, "different watches have different time and [there is] no central time."[37] To Nevin this indicates a tendency toward historical relativism that Babbitt will not openly admit. Relativism, however, does not necessarily mean chaos; there can be an order to things that simply appears differently from different points of view. What Nevin calls Babbitt's "penchant for dualizing a personality into historically defective yet contemporaneously wholesome aspects"[38] is a case in point. Nevin cannot understand, for example, how Babbitt logically can deplore Blaise Pascal's adherence to the doctrines of predestination and innate depravity and at the same time admire his "sense of a principle of superiority in man to the monstrous, blind forces of nature."[39] This "sense of the heart," this grace, Pascal's recognition of which Babbitt so admires, is for Nevin inextricable from Pascal's skepticism and blind faith and therefore antithetical to decorum and the principles of balance Babbitt relies upon. Babbitt knows this, of course. In *Rousseau and Romanticism* he says, "Pascal sees in decorum a disguise of one's ordinary self rather than a real curb upon it, and feels that the gap is not sufficiently wide between even the best type of man of the world and the mere worldling" (*R*, 24).

Unfortunately, Nevin's perspective allows him to grasp only the logical contradiction; he assumes an "either/or" that surely must have forced Babbitt to stare into the "abyss" of historical relativism, only to snatch himself back. Nevin cites another passage from Babbitt's notes on Pascal as the record of this recoiling glimpse: "Have made painful discovery that looking glass faces render back the mental lineaments of the man who consults them."[40] But if this passage is the record of a glimpse into the possibility of meaningless subjectivity, Babbitt certainly does not recoil into using "terms as argumentative conveniences rather than conceptual blocks,"[41] as Nevin claims. In fact, this, the choice between mere rhetoric and mere dialectic, is the either/or from which Babbitt truly recoils. What Nevin fails to recognize is Babbitt's consistent attention to historical changes in concepts. If Nevin had read the very next paragraph in *Rousseau and Romanticism,* the one after Babbitt notes Pascal's rejection of decorum, he would have found that Babbitt's response to Pascal is the following warning: "One should not however, . . . judge of decorum by what it degenerated into" (*R*, 24).

Nevin's criticism assumes that a philosophical position should never shift and that the terms employed from that position should be allowed only one possible meaning. Babbitt's appraisal of Pascal makes good sense if one grants him his belief that words retain only a central core of meaning through history while receiving divergent applications in varying contexts. That is how a tradition endures through changing circumstances. Thus from Babbitt's perspective, it is quite legitimate to defend Pascal's denunciation of an aberrant decorum and yet insist on his fundamentally humanistic temperament. After all, his "sense of the heart" countered a prevailing Cartesian rationalism. It is equally legitimate for Babbitt, from his own perspective, to abhor the doctrine of predestination and innate depravity associated with Pascal's grace while asserting his version of the same doctrine.

In his philosophical criticism Babbitt employed at least three very different perspectives. One provides internal critiques that examine the logical coherence of philosophical positions observed in isolation. A second offers contextual critiques that examine the same positions as responses to local, contemporary situations. Finally, once a position's relative direction has been determined—either as furthering or countering an extremist tendency—a third perspective allows critiques in terms of "universal" standards, that is, in terms of the position's relationship to the entire tradition. The master of such multiple perspectives, for Babbitt, was Charles-Augustin Sainte-Beuve:

In Sainte-Beuve, if anywhere, is found the triumph of that historical second-sight on which the nineteenth century prided itself. Sainte-Beuve was aided in his art of mediating between the past and the present by the "moment": he lived at a time when it was still possible to receive a living initiation into tradition, that is to say, to see the past as it saw itself, which means in practice to live in a world of absolute values; it was already possible, on the other hand, to detach one's self from the past and to see it relatively and phenomenally. This art of mediating between the past and the present is becoming more difficult for us today. We tend to see the past only relatively. . . . (M, 148–49)

Thus, although historical research is necessary if the critic or philosopher is to "distinguish between essence and accident," historical research for its own sake will "fix our attention almost exclusively on . . . local and relative elements" (R, 15). The humanist must always remember that his chief aim is to establish standards that must be tested against those inclinations that all men always have. These inclinations or "elements" of human nature inform the conventions that underlie language. It is important, therefore, to retrieve the common element that may have motivated men to use a particular term in different ways and in different situations.

To achieve this goal, Babbitt recommends that the humanist employ the Socratic standard, which demands that "a definition must not be abstract and metaphysical, but experimental; it must not, that is, reflect our opinion of what a word should mean, but what it actually has meant" (R, 1). Such definition requires a two-part process: "The first step is to perceive the something that connects two or more of these things [main uses of a word] apparently so diverse, and then it may be found necessary to refer this unifying trait itself back to something still more general, and so on until we arrive, not indeed at anything absolute—the absolute will always

elude us—but at what Goethe calls the original or underlying phenomenon (*Urphänomen*)" (*R, 2*). The second step is "to discriminate
between things that are apparently similar" (*R, 2*). In Babbitt's
hands this simple process becomes extraordinarily labored and involved. *Rousseau and Romanticism,* for example, devotes most of its
pages to elaborately defining the terms *romantic* and *classic.* Babbitt
believed that "in an age of sophistry, like the present, criticism
itself amounts largely to that art of inductive defining which it is
the great merit of Socrates, according to Aristotle, to have devised
and brought to perfection" (*R, 374*).

But if Socrates perfected the technique of inductive definition,
Babbitt extended its application. Like Socrates, he tested the value
of concepts as ideal ends for human action against the realities of
historical situations and the "common factors" of human nature.
Unlike Socrates, Babbitt turned inductive definition into a powerful
tool for interpreting texts. Once Babbitt discovers the "unifying
trait" among the meanings a word has been made to carry throughout
a period of history, he uses that trait as a point of measure. Through
a process of comparison and contrast, by defining a peculiar meaning
of a term in a text, he also inductively determines the attitude or
motive that may have allowed an author to apply that term in a
way that earlier authors would not have.

A brief example of this process is found in one of Babbitt's
discussions of the romantic preference for self-expression. He notes
that the word "character" applies to elements in a man's nature.
But the "word character . . . is ambiguous, inasmuch as it may
refer either to the idiosyncratic or to the universal human element
in a man's dual nature" (*R, 47*). A comment Blake makes on Aristotle's use of the term reveals the contrast between the two writers'
attitudes: " 'Aristotle,' he complains, 'says characters are either good
or bad; now Goodness or Badness has nothing to do with Character.
An apple tree, a pear tree, a horse, a lion are Characters; but a good
apple tree or a bad is an apple tree still, etc.' " (*R, 47*). Babbitt
claims that Blake "cannot even understand" the Aristotelian usage
which "implies something that man possesses and that a horse or a
tree does not possess—the power namely to deliberate and choose"
(*R, 47*).

In this case, as in many others like it, the difference in the way
the two authors particularize the general, unifying trait of an important word reveals a more encompassing difference between the

authors' understandings of the proper ends of human thought and action. Aristotle values the self that a man "possesses in common with other men," the self that is capable of choosing among the various alternatives that his society offers him; Blake values the "temperamental or private self," the urges and inclinations that diverge from the norm of his society (*R,* 47).

Inductive definition of this sort serves as a kind of empirical grounding for Babbitt's interpretive claims. Although he consistently denies that a term's historically constant core trait can be considered its absolute or "true meaning," such unifying traits nevertheless represent for him a certain stability within language, which he acknowledges is always changing. The broad claims he makes about the meaning of an author's work—as when he says that the "contrast between nature and convention is indeed almost the whole of Rousseauism"—always emerge from inductive definitions of important terms, important in that they are central to an author's work and that the terms deviate significantly from historical usage. From such definitions Babbitt infers a more general, controlling attitude or set of attitudes, and these he takes to define the author's work. Through a further series of comparisons he classifies an author historically. Rousseauism, for example, is a kind of romanticism that contrasts sharply with neoclassicism, that influences modernism, and that resembles utilitarianism more than one might think.

Babbitt's writing moves continually back and forth hermeneutically from the attitudes governing the usage of a particular word in a particular context to the more general definitions of global movements. His philosophical arguments take place, of course, at the higher levels of generalization when he contrasts the values of romanticism against those of classicism: genius against imitation, expression against form. Opposing concepts such as these, although apparently confined to literature, in the large sense of the term, have practical, sometimes devastating consequences for the political, the educational, and the cultural life of the community and the individual. If the history of literature appears as a continual swaying from one extreme formulation of language to another, the history of human action swings along with it. The true humanist, rare though he may be, attempts always to mediate between the extremes, to bring the half-truth of one into line with the half-truth of the other. Even when he is successful, the balance is tentative and must be regained as circumstances alter, as the pressures of everyday life change.

Babbitt's interpretative method and his philosophy of discipline and mediation, as chapters 4, 5, and 6 will show, form and justify his views of literary theory, education, politics, and religion. As chapter 3 will demonstrate, the concept of mediation also affected the way Babbitt and his disciples would present humanism to the world. More so than most intellectual movements, the history of humanism is largely the result of a conscious strategy, one that was only partially successful, but one that nevertheless acknowledged that ideas must live in a world of action and circumstance.

Chapter Three
The Humanist Campaign

In the first two decades of the twentieth century Harvard was a place of extremes; students could join the most snobbish clubs or express their revolutionary spirit in the Harvard Socialist Society. During this period Harvard turned out many of the poets who would constitute the high modernist movement—Wallace Stevens, Conrad Aiken, E. E. Cummings—as well as many of the young intellectuals who would lead the assault on America's political and cultural institutions—Walter Lippmann, Van Wyck Brooks, John Reed. At the same time, hundreds of students flocked to hear Professor Bliss Perry celebrate American idealism in his surveys of American literature.[1] Some Harvard students, however, could neither wholeheartedly celebrate America nor attack it in the cause of a new intellectual and moral liberation. Among such young men, Babbitt found a growing audience.

The Saving Remnant Gathers

In 1910 Babbitt had about eighty advanced students in all his five classes. Eventually he would be holding single classes in an auditorium seating over three hundred. His appeal, it seems, was more than the high seriousness of his subject. William Maag recalls him as "the only teacher I ever had who constantly enlivened his lectures with wit and humor, or thought that fun had a definite place in class."[2] Eventually, he became one of Harvard's "characters," like Kittredge himself, whose performances were not to be missed.

On a typical day Babbitt would enter the classroom carrying a green felt book bag stuffed full. He would march directly to his table at the front of the room, sit down, and disgorge his notes and books, each having perhaps dozens of slips of paper protruding to mark relevant passages. After entertaining questions about the previous lecture, he would begin his torrential outpouring of ideas. At any point he was likely to pause dramatically and, to hoots from the class, with great showmanship announce "I choose an illustration at random." Whatever the example, it usually expressed some human foible that startled the whole class into laughter, in which he heartily joined. If, for instance, he were discussing the romantic infatuation with the "beautiful soul," he might cite Rousseau or Renan, but he was as likely to plunge into his notes and extract a clipping from the day's newspaper about the thief who excused his crimes because "the proceeds of his recent robberies have been used to educate two orphan girls who befriended him in England." Besides referring to the many texts and clippings he brought to class, he drew upon his amazing memory. He was able to call forth so many references that his students began conducting betting pools to see how many authors he would mention in a single fifty-minute lecture. The record seems to be seventy-five.[3]

In 1902 he began teaching many of his courses in the newly founded Department of Comparative Literature, though he had as little sympathy for the other comparatists as he had for his colleagues in the Department of French. He never considered himself engaged in an archeological expedition; Rousseau and Bacon were living presences in the minds of foolish modern men and women. He scoffed at the idea that a philologist, William Henry Schofield, could head a comparative literature department, for Schofield had "never done anything literary" and viewed literature as the "mere *relative* product of the circumstances of time and space." The right kind of comparatist, Babbitt felt, grasps "the absolute human element that binds together the men of different periods." Babbitt wanted to "escape from the quicksands of relativity to some firm ground of judgment." In class, he therefore largely ignored the chronological tracing of derivations and influences and ransacked the literatures of the world to illustrate the absolute elements in human nature. T. S. Eliot, a graduate student under Babbitt in 1909-1910, recalls, "Superficially, his lectures were almost without method. . . . [B]eginning anywhere and ending anywhere, he gave us the impression that a life-time was too short for telling us all that he wanted to say. The lectures which I attended were concerned with French Literary Criticism; but they had a good deal to do with Aristotle, Longinus, and Dionysius of Helicarnassus . . . [,with] Buddhism, Confucius, Rousseau, and contemporary political and

religious movements." And from the firm ground of his understanding of human nature, Babbitt passed few positive judgments
on the literature he surveyed.[4]

Although his wit attracted scores of students, Babbitt always
employed it for serious purposes. In the first meeting of Comp Lit
II (the Romantic Movement in the Nineteenth Century) he assured
his students he would impose no orthodoxy, but he warned them
they would not be gushing over the beauties of Keats or Shelley
either. Defining romanticism fully, he told them, was "like building
a bridge across chaos." Consequently, they would avoid an ency-
clopedic presentation of facts on the one hand and a close study of
individual authors on the other. They would concern themselves
with only "one type of romanticism and in one main aspect," the
"attempt of this type of romanticism to offer the equivalent of ethics
and religion."[5] Having established this narrow focus, Babbitt spent
the rest of the course pointing out the disastrous consequences of
this attempt and upholding his humanist principles.

As Babbitt grew older, his arthritic stoop increased, and he developed a shambling gait. White hair and jowls gave him a bulldog
look, and his call for questions often produced silence from the
terrified class. In his last years questions usually elicited an unil-
luminating summary of what had been said before, and any student
who mixed up the facts was likely to get his head snapped off.
Throughout his career his lack of evident method was likely to
befuddle indolent undergraduates. "Say," one supposedly muttered
to his neighbor in the sixth month of the year, "what's this course
all about, anyhow?" Even graduate students he had converted tended
to find him closed-minded, to consider his ideas "labeled and clas-
sified and put in their places with an almost mechanical, if vigorous,
efficiency."[6] Four decades of classifying every person or idea as
humanistic or humanitarian had, it seems, made it all too easy to
see only these categories.

Nevertheless, the humanist movement began in Babbitt's classroom. He asserted a moral authority hard to come by elsewhere,
and his ideas exerted a far-reaching influence for decades to come.
The experience of Austin Warren, a leading theorist of the New
Criticism that dominated American critical thought from the 1930s
to the 1970s, was perhaps typical. Warren came to Babbitt's graduate courses from a small college whose senior English professor was
"a cultivated gentleman in frockcoat and sidewhiskers." At Harvard,

Warren was bewildered at first by the massive, powerful, "leoninely restless" man who seemed anything but a genteel exponent of high culture and who "was addressing his blows, thrusts, thumps at some unseen assailant, some enemy . . . threatening the disruption of civilization." Eventually, Warren's boyish enthusiasms faded until, "Though I could not tell day and hour, I, like so very many others in that academic campground, experienced conversion."[7]

Besides Paul Elmer More, who had been issuing a steady stream of essays and books since the late 1890s, several of Babbitt's students were, by 1920, beginning to spread humanist ideas. At the University of Illinois, Stuart Sherman published his first two books in 1917: *Matthew Arnold: How to Know Him* (largely a statement of the humanist position) and *On Contemporary Literature* (an all-out assault on the works Babbitt himself scarcely deigned to notice). With his caustic wit, Sherman, playing on anti-German sentiment, attacked the "barbaric naturalism" of Theodore Dreiser, as well as other contemporaries, and relished the howls he elicited from his opponents. "It shows . . . that we have got under their skins," he wrote More in 1918.[8]

At the University of North Carolina, Norman Foerster carried on the fight in his classrooms. In 1919 he assured Babbitt that "More and more I am directly using my 'creed' (in nearly all essentials your creed) in my teaching, with vitalizing results. . . . Few of our students are naturalistic; most of them are still living in a pre-Darwinian era—the old religion and morality. My task . . . is to make them modern in the best sense."[9] Foerster would play a central role in the literary wars of the next decade and would carry the campaign into the thirties with books such as *Towards Standards* (1930) and *The Future of the Liberal Arts College* (1938).

In England T. S. Eliot called for a new poetry based on the ideas of his former teacher. In his 1919 "Tradition and the Individual Talent," he echoed the master in calling for "depersonalization" in art instead of romantic self-expression and in urging poets to live in "the present moment of the past." Years later, referring to his student days, Eliot asserted that "If one has once had that relationship with Babbitt, he remains permanently an active influence."[10] Although Babbitt was struck by the remarkable discrepancy between Eliot's theory and practice (*The Waste Land* suggesting the fragmented modern sensibility much more than classical wholeness and proportion), he appreciated an ally abroad.

At Bowdoin (later at Amherst) G. R. Elliott also enlisted in the cause. Though never actually Babbitt's student, he was impressed by Babbitt's and More's books. Having one day sneaked into Babbitt's Harvard classroom, he wrote "since meeting you I have been thinking much of your sense of the need of more cooperation among the forces of criticism in this country. . . . I wish you would state your view publicly. . . . You might thus touch the consciences of many remote collegiate persons scattered through this country who, like me, are . . . romanticists somewhat tempered by reflection and renunciation."[11]

Elliott did not realize that for two decades Babbitt had been attempting to forge just such a cooperative effort. The last thing Babbitt wanted, however, was to lead a romantic crusade or to have humanism lumped with Imagism, Socialism, Progressivism, Freudianism, or any of the other proliferating "isms" of the time. He believed himself engaged in a war for the survival of civilization and wanted a body of dedicated men—a "keen–sighted few" or a "saving remnant"—willing to subordinate their passions to a calculated strategy.[12]

An Unexpected Flanking Movement

Early in his career, while battling the philological syndicate for survival at Harvard, Babbitt found it "disheartening to stand out almost alone against the main drift of one's time." Thomas Nevin suggests that Babbitt was exhilarated by assuming the stance of the lonely fighter.[13] As chapter 1 shows, he certainly seems to have enjoyed being the lone gun, but he also longed to be a part of the comitatus, to feel what Stephen Crane called "the subtle battle brotherhood."

As early as 1908 Babbitt had admonished More for giving a poor review to a potential ally, Hall Frye: "There are several of us who stand for somewhat similar ideas in education and literature . . . but I fear that we are not showing much practical shrewdness in our team play." Usually, however, Babbitt chose a military metaphor; for example, he characterized a 1915 address to Harvard's Philosophical Club as "carry[ing] the warfare into the enemy's country." The metaphor could be a private joke among the humanists, as when Elliott addressed his letters to Babbitt "Dear General."[14] However, it also expressed a sense of common purpose and self-sacrifice and fostered a serious concern for tactics, a concern that deeply influenced the form of the typical humanist argument.

Babbitt, for instance, advised More to limit references to *Literature and the American College* in a forthcoming article to a single objective footnote written "as it might have been if you had never known me." The purpose apparently was to avoid, as More had put it, the "mutual puffing" that would make the movement seem less than a spontaneous efflorescence of the classical spirit. And when his own books were being excoriated by hostile reviewers, Babbitt thought it "good tactics" for new writers with humanistic leanings not to mention him at all so they could get a fair hearing. [15]

Babbitt's most important tactic was his effort to meet science on its own ground, something More's Platonic idealism could not do. In 1912 he wrote More that, although a Platonic "line of attack" could be effective against romanticism, it was open to "romantic parody"; he preferred Aristotle's emphasis on experience "because it does not lend itself to such subtle and baffling perversions." A few years later he accused More of a worse tactical error: in a 1916 essay on "Natural Aristocracy" More admitted to being a kind of Tory. Babbitt realized that such an admission would only hurt the cause in an age proud of its modernism: "To admit at present that one is a Tory or even a reactionary is in my opinion to commit a tactical mistake of the first order. One is at once put on the defensive; and in the war of intellect . . . the advantage belongs with the offensive. . . ."[16]

Babbitt proposed "an unexpected flanking movement" that would take the enemy off guard. Humanists should deny their dependence on the past; they should try to out-modern the moderns, particularly the scientific naturalists. If they defined the modern spirit as "positive and critical," they could accuse the scientists of "more than mediaeval credulity" for believing in fictions like the ether or the atom, purely imaginary constructs no one had ever experienced. If the humanists insisted on a positive and critical method in defining natural law, they could claim a similar method in defining human law. "One should plant himself first of all here on the naked *fact* of a power of control in human nature," he advised More. Only then would it be proper to call upon the "collateral testimony" of the sages.

This is not to say that emphasizing humanism's positive and critical side was a mere tactic. The psychological fact of a higher will, or power of control, was the bedrock on which the humanist edifice was constructed and goes back to Babbitt's readings in Buddhism in the 1880s and 1890s. However, in his early works Babbitt had been most concerned with strengthening the "links in that unbroken chain of literary and intellectual tradition which extends from the ancient to the modern world." Beginning with *Rousseau and Romanticism* (1919), his most devastating weapon was his insistence that only the humanists truly embodied the modern spirit. Arguing that the "whole modern experiment is threatened with breakdown simply because it has not been sufficiently modern," he presented a creed "so modern that, compared with it, that of our smart young radicals will seem antediluvian." And he could always, of course, count on collateral testimony from the great "positive and critical" minds of the past—those of professors Aristotle and Buddha. [17]

Other humanists followed Babbitt's lead. In the *Demon of the Absolute* (1928) More insisted that modern science demanded "the same sort of credulity as was demanded of the theologian in the Middle Ages when asked to debate the number of angels who could stand together on the point of a needle." And when the humanists issued their 1930 manifesto, *Humanism and America,* neither Babbitt nor More supplied the lead article; that honor went to More's brother Louis, a physicist who no doubt was supposed to lend the whole manifesto scientific authority. Louis too ridiculed the fictions of science, equating modern experimental psychology with astrology and calling the new theories of Einstein and Whitehead "as nonsensical as the hallucinations of the mediaeval monk driven mad by the fevers of asceticism." [18] In these attacks the humanists hoped to establish the psyche as their own domain and to show that science held no greater claim to objective truth than did their own "common sense" or observations of subjective states.

A Failure to Communicate

Until the late 1920s humanism remained the lonely cause of Babbitt's saving remnant. The most obvious reason was the mood of the country. For many intellectuals after the war, the civilization the humanists revered was just "an old bitch gone in the teeth," as Ezra Pound phrased it. Many of those intellectuals the humanists most needed to reach were caught up in hedonism, in attacks on

"Puritanism," and in the religion of art. As for the general public, the 1920s were a boom time in which business was king. Even Jesus, according to Bruce Barton's best-seller *The Man Nobody Knew*, was a super-executive who "picked up twelve men from the bottom ranks of business and forged them into an organization that conquered the world." Everywhere values of the past were denied. Henry Ford was speaking for a whole generation when he said "History is more or less bunk."[19]

Still, Babbitt would have reached a wider audience if he had made his ideas more accessible. After reading the manuscript of Babbitt's 1917 article "Interpreting India to the West," More criticized his friend for hiding "the rigid cold syllogism under a mass of allusion and illustration." Babbitt responded defensively that if he had "syllogized" his argument he "should have been thrown out of Harvard."[20] The truth is, Babbitt simply did not possess a coldly syllogistic mind.

His real medium of expression was always the spoken word—the more extemporaneous the better. Even when giving formal public lectures, such as the 1922 Phi Beta Kappa address at Northwestern, he avoided a prepared text because "I have found that it is not possible to establish contact with an audience when one keeps one's nose in a manuscript."[21] Before publishing his ideas he preached them for years in his classes and lectures. In reading through his classroom notes, one constantly encounters the phrases that appear in books written many years later. In a sense, *Rousseau and Romanticism* is merely Comp Lit 9 in hardback.

Although he was one of the most literate men of his age, his attitude toward truth was more like that of someone raised in an oral culture. He believed that knowledge must be seized by the intuition, not the analytical intellect, and he relied heavily upon the aphorism and the epigram because they made his ideas easy to remember. His lectures often came across "in periods about the length of an epigram," and he most enjoyed "thumping out a couplet."[22] When he felt ready to bring his ideas together in a book, he would write a rough draft, very rapidly, often breaking off in mid-sentence, as one does in speaking, to pursue a new line of thought. (He had trained himself to write with both hands so that he could write for hours on end without stopping.) Later drafts were even more like oral performances. Indeed, they were oral performances, for he dictated from his rough draft as Dora wrote out his

words in longhand. Only then would he send the manuscript off to
More for comment and concern himself with the niceties of written
English.

For *Democracy and Leadership* (originally to be called *Democracy and
Imperialism*), he seems to have worked outward from a series of
aphorisms to the book's larger structures. His notes in the Babbitt
Papers at Harvard consist of many small sheets torn from bluebooks,
each containing a single idea with no context. They show his
striving for compression and balance and frequently relying on antithesis, alliteration, and rhyme as aids to memory:

Those who like W. J. Bryan turn Jesus from a prince of peace into a
prince of pacifism.

It may be that the net result of our failure to believe in a future hell [in
a] world to come will be to get our hell in this world.

Man wants flattery, he needs criticism; he needs conversion, he wants
diversion; he wants power, he needs peace.

With such aphorisms as a kernel, Babbitt apparently deposited
layers of more expository prose and examples drawn from all manner
of sources until he had enough material for a lecture. The problem
was providing coherence to a string of these separate pearls. More
was exasperated with his friend's tendency to rely on the aphorism
instead of a full, logical argument. He complained of the "rotary
movement" of Babbitt's prose and his inclination "to crowd his
whole thesis, at least implicitly, into each single paragraph, so that
the book, despite the inexhaustible variety of his illustrations, gives
the impression of endless repetition."[23] To those for whom his
aphorisms tallied with the chant of their souls, Babbitt was a true
prophet. To others, especially those who had never felt his charis-
matic attraction in person, he was an ill-tempered moralist suffering
from a poverty of ideas.

Babbitt's circularity, his seemingly endless illustration of a few
ideas, and his love for the aphorism remind one faintly of Emerson,
though Babbitt's style lacks the sonorities of the Concord sage's.
Emerson's style, too, had its roots in orality—the Unitarian sermon
with its use of copious illustration and the witty conversations of
the Transcendentalists.[24] Those who knew Babbitt well, however,

always equated him with another great speaker—Samuel Johnson. W. K. Wimsatt has called Johnson's style "a way of saying the same thing over and over," a phrase that applies equally to Babbitt's. Furthermore, Johnson relied heavily on tight antithetical constructions reminiscent of Babbitt's aphorisms:

Dryden knew more of man in his general nature, and Pope in his local manners.

Dryden is read with frequent astonishment, and Pope with perpetual delight.

For both Johnson and Babbitt, antithesis creates problems when it becomes a larger structural pattern; the result is often a retraction or cancellation of the intended meaning.[25] Babbitt seldom passes judgment without almost immediately establishing an opposite, contradictory point of view:

Burke is usually and rightly supposed to embody the spirit of moderation. Many of his utterences on the French Revolution, however . . ., are scarcely suggestive of moderation. . . .[26]

Greece is perhaps the most humane of countries. . . . The majority at any particular instant in Greece or elsewhere is almost sure to be unsound. . . . (*LC,* 24)

The points of contact between [Confucius's] doctrine and that of Aristotle . . . are numerous and striking. . . . [O]ne should hasten to add that in their total attitude towards life they reveal the characteristic difference between the European and the Asiatic temper. (*DL,* 163–64)

This continual hastening to add qualifications stems in large part from Babbitt's philosophy of balance and mediation. Nevertheless, it contributes to a general fuzziness. Seeming to take back almost every assertion, he contributes to his books' rotary effect by leaving his readers practically where they started, a problem compounded by the personality Babbitt projected in his books.

This last problem relates to the satirical intention behind much of his writing. Babbitt was amused as well as outraged by America's absurdities. In one of his typical lectures he followed up a serious

denunciation of America's lack of standards with hilarious examples
of the average American's taste for the bizarre as revealed in the
headlines of the daily papers:

Freaks hunger while men fight to feed them; six-legged cow dies

Kink in pup's tail leads to murder

Negro, aged 112, retains optimism as wife drops dead at his feet[27]

He thus shared his enemy H. L. Mencken's delight in ridiculing
the "booboisie." He also sympathized with some of the more serious
satires of democratic mediocrity, such as Sinclair Lewis's *Main Street*
and Edgar Lee Masters's *Spoon River Anthology.*

Neither Lewis nor Masters, however, provided the right kind of
satire in Babbitt's view. Satire, he argued, "must be constructive"
and show Main Street "on a background of standards" (*DL,* 262).
And as he warned More, who had associated the humanist critical
spirit with the more malicious satires of Pope, "it is in my judgment
a tactical error to seem to identify the critical and satirical spirit
with malice." Great satirists like Boileau, Horace, and Johnson had
all managed to produce keen satire that was "genial rather than
malicious."[28] His own works, he apparently believed, were just the
kind of genial satire on a background of standards that could serve
as a corrective to America's vices.

Babbitt did not recognize that all satire seems malicious to the
victim. The readers he wanted to reach—humanitarians, philologists, scientists—found their deepest convictions ridiculed in the
pages of his books, which sometimes seem intended more to delight
the converted than to convert the unenlightened. Nowhere are Babbitt's satirical intentions more evident than in his first book.

In the preface to *Literature and the American College* Babbitt announces that "my aim has been to define types and tendencies, and
not to satirize or even label individuals" (vii). He "makes no claim
to completeness" (viii) in his treatment of persons living or dead,
but will expose those single facets of character that serve his purposes. In this he takes the traditional stance of the satirist: I will
hold a mirror up to the age to expose its evils; if you see your own
reflection I am not to blame. He names his two basic character types
"Bacon" and "Rousseau" to remove his definitions of scientific and

sentimental humanitarians "from the cloud-land of abstraction" and to make them "concrete and historical" (35). Bacon and Rousseau are monsters, not only "great forerunners of the future" but also "men of weak and in some respects contemptible character" (38). Having established these types of human monstrosity, Babbitt parades scores of their successors across the reader's field of vision. Like the scene of traditional satire described by Alvin Kernan, the book is "disorderly and crowded, packed to the very point of bursting. The deformed faces of depravity, stupidity, greed, venality, ignorance, and maliciousness group closely together for a moment, stare boldly out at us, break up, and another tight knot of figures collects. . . ."[29]

Human deformity appears most frequently in the eighth chapter, "On Being Original," which argues that the man who usually passes for being original "is in reality only freakish" (215). Among Babbitt's freaks (and this list is very partial) are Petrarch, who cultivated his own peculiarities and called for liberty merely as "a cloak for license" (218); the seventeenth-century Marinists and euphuists, who have "all the nodosities of the oak without its strength" (219); the modern artists who are "inbreeding personal and national peculiarities" (219–20); the neoclassicists like Rymer who set up "servile imitation" as an ideal (220); Rousseau himself, who is merely a "self-torturing sophist" (222); Emerson, who encouraged "nightmare originalities" (225); the modernist "who poses and attitudinizes" before the world (225); Baudelaire, who had a "pathological" aversion to normal human behavior (229); modern writers who dwell "on the remote periphery of human nature" (232); Hugo, who wrote "Cyclopean" works (232); the revisionist historians who reject "the traditional good sense of the world" (235); the university professors who pursue research "too eccentric and centrifugal" to be valuable (238).

This chapter pushes the limits of geniality. Readers hear, in fact, the voice of the traditional satirical persona standing within what Kernan calls satire's "dense and grotesque world of decaying matter moving without form in response only to physical forces and denying the humane ideal which once molded the crowd into a society." In contrast to the monsters inhabiting this world, the satirist is always a blunt, no-nonsense type, pessimistic about man's future but driven by Juvenal's *saeva indignatio* (savage indignation) to speak out against evil. As the last spokesman for a lost ideal, he assumes heroic postures, "the only champion of virtue who dares to speak the truth in a world where the false insolently maintains itself as the real."[30]

The Irving Babbitt of *Literature and the American College* stands for the good cause; as one of the few "men of ideas" (147), he lives the ideal of "high, impersonal reason" (174) while the rest of the world is given over to emotionalism and fact collecting. He views this world with indignation and "intellectual nausea" (134) as it slips into "brutal naturalism" (63) and holds out little hope for its resurrection. His kind of life is inevitably a lonely heroic struggle against great odds: "The humanist who at present enters college teaching should not underestimate the difficulties he is likely to encounter. . . . [He] will have to undertake the task . . . of creating the taste by which he is to be enjoyed. He will be more or less out of touch with his colleagues; and, though he will attract some students of the more serious sort, will not necessarily win wide and sudden popularity. . . ." (144–45).

Paradoxically, however, the virtuous satirist often, through the rigor of his attack, opens himself to charges of intemperance, pride, and self-righteousness. As a result, satirists from Juvenal to Swift have been vilified when they have merely created the kinds of personas necessitated by their form.

Babbitt's thrusts against the "philological syndicate" did not suggest moderation and geniality, nor did his Swiftean caricatures, such as "the Chicago professor who recently spent a year in collecting cats'-cradles on the Congo" (a true descendant of Swift's "projectors" who tried to extract sunbeams from cucumbers [*LC,* 31]). He openly admired the "aloofness and disdain" (*LC,* 17) of Castiglione's Courtier and when accused of intolerance would simply reply that there was no room for compromise on first principles. As one might expect, his opponents took him to be an arrogant, prudish, rigid authoritarian who lacked sympathy for the pains and desires of his fellowman. His friends, though, attested to his magnanimity in privately admitting the virtues of his opponents—even Rousseau and Kittredge—and attributed to his books an admirably decorous restraint. His opponents were partly wrong because they mistook the satirist for the man. But his friends were only partly right. For Babbitt was a decorous critic of modernism only when compared with the other combatants. The literary wars of the 1920s might not have been hell, but neither were they notable for chivalry.

Bleeding for the Cause

An important means of carrying on the fight was the judiciously placed review, laudatory of the humanists' works and critical of the enemy's. The Babbitt-More correspondence is filled with discussions of reviews and advice on where best to place articles for effect. When More's review of *Rousseau and Romanticism* was rejected by the *Unpartizan,* Babbitt suggested several alternative journals and even asked that More send it to him first: "With the help of the women of the family I can probably arrive at a fairly accurate estimate. Parts may deserve to be salvaged. . . ." (What wouldn't any author give to be able to edit reviews of his own books!) He then offered to help More write an article portraying humanism as an international movement; in that way, More "might do something . . . that would command attention in important quarters."[31]

Reviewing nonhumanist books like Joel Spingarn's *Creative Criticism* could bring out Babbitt's less magnanimous side. "Spingarn," he wrote More, "is a dangerous anarchist. He is one of those who . . . need to bleed for the good of the cause." In his review he accused Spingarn of a primitivism "repugnant to the most elementary common sense" and hinted strongly at a link between Spingarn's theory of genius and German imperialism. Ironically, besides drawing blood, the review occasioned one of the few gentlemanly acts associated with the humanist controversy. Spingarn, then an infantry officer training for combat, wrote Babbitt a gracious letter thanking him sincerely for the "learning, culture, and courtesy" displayed in the review even though Spingarn disagreed with almost every sentence.[32] This spirit of chivalry was not to survive the Great War.

Just as the frantic hedonism of the 1920s reached its height, and the Big Bull Market began the incredible inflation of stock prices, the humanists began to find an audience for their ideas. One commentator sympathetic to the humanists announced that at last the liberals had "to forsake their accustomed olympianism" as "all the sad young men, futile, frustrate and skeptic, [began] casting off their grave clothes and trooping after prophets who talk to them of Tradition and Authority!"[33] Journals with humanist leanings began to publish frequent articles promoting the cause, most notably the *Hound and the Horn,* edited by Bernard Bandler, and the *Bookman,* edited by Seward Collins. Attacks came from both the left and right, from liberal journals like the *Nation* and *New Republic* and right-wing journals like H. L. Mencken's *American Mercury*. In England T. S. Eliot's *Criterion* gave a hearing to all views.

Both sides were guilty of vicious smear tactics. Mencken scoffed at Babbitt as the "Bishop Cannon" of a humanism best viewed as "a somewhat sickly and shame-faced Christian mysticism." Babbitt in turn dismissed Mencken's criticism as "intellectual vaudeville." When More referred in passing to John Dos Passos's *Manhattan Transfer* as "an explosion in a cesspool," he stirred a number of outraged replies. One that Babbitt undoubtedly took as evidence of a palpable hit was a shrill letter from Upton Sinclair to Seward Collins: "I am going to enter my plea against your turning the 'Bookman' into a propaganda organ for those two literary mummies, More and Babbitt. One or two articles about them is all right, but month after month, causes us to stop reading."[34]

The most venomous attacks, however, came from Seward Collins, a champion of humanist "moderation." In responding to Edmund Wilson's unfavorable review of *Humanism and America,* Collins exceeded all bounds of taste. Wilson's article was "the most disgraceful" of all the "silly and petty and nasty performances" of the humanists' enemies: "It is doubtful, indeed, whether American literature had ever before seen so shocking an example of pure malevolence supported by ignorance in essential matters, by blundering obtuseness, and by complete abdication of conscience both personal and professional." Such a diatribe smacks of fascist hysteria, and Collins indeed moved on from humanism to champion Mussolini. As Alter Brody put it in the *New Republic,* in Collins's articles humanism "emerges as the intellectual program of the Boston Chapter of the Daughters of the American Revolution, differing from the Ku Klux Klan by being more exclusive."[35]

Dissension in the Ranks

Although the intemperance of a hanger-on like Seward Collins was damaging to the humanist cause, Babbitt himself began to gain an increasing amount of national and international recognition: he was elected to the National Institute of Arts and Letters in 1920 and to the American Academy of Arts and Letters in 1930. But he gained the most satisfaction from his election in 1926 as a corresponding member of the French Institute, an extremely rare honor for an American. Finally, he believed, he had found the respect in the international intellectual community that had been denied him by his own colleagues at Harvard. However, his sense of personal satisfaction was undercut by a series of defections from the movement—by far the most serious being Paul Elmer More's. Babbitt had always hoped that one day he and More could pursue their close alliance and friendship together at Harvard. He had even tried, with Royce's help, to get More on at Harvard after he left the *Nation* in 1914, but apparently the philologists were not about to allow another humanist on the faculty.[36]

More bought a home near Princeton University, where he continued to write while teaching an occasional course in Hellenistic and early Christian philosophy. By early 1920, Babbitt thought he noticed a "defeatist" attitude in More's letters, just when it was "the time to be more aggressive than ever." Never as combative as the "Warring Buddha of Harvard," More, the "Hermit of Princeton," began to show leanings toward the "Hindu doctrine of detachment" and to accept the fact that he would have little practical influence on his age. It would be enough, he believed, if the humanists could keep the tradition alive for those who followed. Within a couple of years Babbitt was detecting an "extreme holiness" in More's published commentary on Plato's deity. By the time he published *Christ of the New Testament* in 1924, More was far along toward a full acceptance of Christ's divinity. The only escape from modern materialism, he believed, was "the awakening of the sense of . . . otherworldliness."[37]

Babbitt, who wanted a humanism founded on the objective facts of man's nature, accused his friend of "a change of base line" and foresaw that "effective cooperation between us is going to become more difficult." The friendship was too deep to be shattered over a philosophical disagreement, but More became a sympathetic observer rather than a central protagonist in the battle for humanism. And without close philosophical agreement Babbitt could never feel the old sense of communion. For a few brief months in the spring of 1926, when More replaced a Harvard classics professor on leave for one semester, the friendship was restored to something like its original intimacy. Almost every evening Babbitt walked to More's house and renewed his original assault on his friend's otherworld-

liness with "such a stream of argument, invective, and persuasion
as had not, I am sure, been heard in Cambridge before and probably
will bever be heard again. It was *magnifique, et c'était la guerre!*"[38]

The battle was essentially between More's Platonism and Babbitt's
Aristotelianism—as Babbitt put it, between a belief in a transcendent world of ideas and a belief in a human world "dominated by
the idea of work and energy and the closely related idea of end or
purpose." This time More was unmoved. "I can convince the whole
world," Babbitt would shout, brandishing an umbrella as he readied
himself to leave, "but I cannot convince you!" Unruffled, More
would reply, "How about a little cheese?" and the futile struggle
would resume.[39]

Other defections were less serious, but painful all the same. Like
More, both Sherman and Eliot found a pure humanism too austere.
As early as 1917 Sherman, the enfant terrible of the movement,
was beginning to profess a "windy democratic 'idealism' " that left
Babbitt "very cold." Sherman's turn in the early 1920s to a "religion
of democracy" and a celebration of such modern authors as Sherwood
Anderson and Willa Cather, was, More believed and Babbitt no
doubt concurred, "no less than a compact signed with the devil."[40]

Eliot followed More, eventually defining his attitude "as classicist
in literature, royalist in politics, and anglo-catholic in religion."
Babbitt would have fully embraced the first, have sympathized with
the second, but likely have sneered at the third as the "affinity . . .
of the jelly-fish for the rock" (*R, 263*), although in 1923, while
visiting his ex-student in England, he did encourage Eliot to make
his conversion public. Moreover, Babbitt saw an "odd twist" in
Eliot's tendency to admire those who made an art of their lives
regardless of the "fruits" of their ideas. Referring to the collection
For Lancelot Andrewes, Babbitt wrote More that, to read Eliot, one
would think "Machiavelli was a pure and dedicated spirit and Baudelaire not only a classicist but an example of true Christian
humility."[41]

In that same collection Eliot included an essay on Babbitt and
charged humanism with being "parasitical" because it could exist
only in a society with a strong religious heritage, and then only for
a short time. He would contribute to the humanist manifesto in
1930, but only to support humanism as a critical spirit that would
save religion from the "vulgarities" of Roman Catholicism and Protestant fundamentalism.[42]

The Remnant's Last Stand

Despite all the defections, Babbitt was never discouraged for long. In the summer of 1928 he and Dora traveled to Europe for a working vacation (he knew no other kind) that included his only visit to his beloved Greece. Recent months had seen the publication of *Mouvement Humaniste aux États-Unis* by his Harvard colleague Louis J. A. Mercier; *American Criticism,* an anthology edited by Norman Foerster in which he laid out the humanist position more systematically than either Babbitt or More had been able to do; a book on Milton by G. R. Elliott; and a two-part article on Babbitt in *The Nineteenth Century and After.* Encouraged by these publications and by his sojourn at the site of the greatest humanistic flowering the world had known, he began to speak hopefully of a "genuine humanistic movement."[43]

When he returned to America, however, he was at first willing to let others lead the fight. Back in 1924, he had advised Norman Foerster that "It is time for the younger men to take a hand." Now Foerster was doing just that by organizing a manifesto of a dozen or so of the most prominent humanists. Foerster thought it crucial that the collection have contributions from Babbitt and More. More, however, was reluctant, as was Babbitt, both wanting the movement to continue on its own merits. "Humanism is not a one-man nor again a two-man movement," asserted Babbitt, while also claiming a too-busy schedule.[44] He may also have had some doubts about such a structured forum.

By early 1929, however, Babbitt's combative nature was aroused. Having offered to let Foerster republish an older article, he suddenly wrote that he was willing to contribute a new piece entitled "Humanism: An Essay at Definition" and would require as many as ten thousand words to do the job right.[45]

At age sixty-four Babbitt may have feared he was losing his leadership, a new feeling he did not especially relish. When T. S. Eliot attacked *American Criticism,* Babbitt jested to Foerster that "you are stirring up a good many polemics. Indeed, if you continue at the present rate, I shall soon have to be looking to my own laurels in this field." He was not merely jesting. By July he was trying to reassume his generalship in what he had once termed "the 'shock troops' of humanism." No longer did he feel that moderation and cautious tactics were in order. When a friend, after a rousing tennis match, suggested that an organized body of zealots contradicted the ideal of moderation, he snapped, "If the best men want to rescue themselves they will have to come together, support each other, preach a gospel. . . . Everyone must risk lop-sideness in an endeavor to redress the balance we have lost." If the manifesto were to succeed, he became convinced, it would need a full, accurate definition of humanism as "the lynch-pin of the whole performance."[46] He was also convinced he was the man to write it.

Whatever hopes Babbitt may have had that *Humanism and America* would turn the tide of modernism were soon disappointed. Besides his own lynch-pin definition, the collection had some able essays, but the newer converts seemed to add little to the ideas of the older generation. Moreover, the collection prodded the movement's enemies into making a counterstatement, *The Critique of Humanism: A Symposium,* which ridiculed Babbitt et al. as genteel academics and Puritans and accused them of an elitist insensitivity to the sufferings of the average man—a particularly telling thrust as America began to witness the breadlines and Hoovervilles of the Great Depression.

Perhaps hoping that Babbitt's charisma could carry the day, his friends persuaded him to engage his opponents in public discussion. In May 1930, before three thousand people in Carnegie Hall, Babbitt, Henry Seidel Canby, and Carl Van Doren presented their views on the question of humanism. It was a fiasco. The introductory speeches were inept, and malfunctioning amplifiers made Babbitt inaudible because he followed his usual practice of speaking with his head down except for emphatic points. All he rescued from the occasion was a bitter joke at his own expense. "Though it was a very warm day," he told his friend Theodore Spencer, "the occasion might be described as a frost."[47]

Babbitt was probably not surprised that the humanists' efforts to reach a broad popular audience were wasted. He perhaps experienced his first doubts when Foerster urged him to delete the phrase "the humanist Erasmus" in his essay's first sentence so that "plain readers" would not be put off. And he must have cringed when Farrar and Rinehart, publishers of *Humanism and America,* pushed the book in the *Saturday Review of Literature* as a spiritual nostrum: "Is this the philosophy for YOU to live by in the 20th Century? Is the famous 'inner check' of the Humanists the answer to the chaos of our times? Only *you* can decide. . . ."[48]

As far as the average American was concerned, humanism turned out after all to be just another fad—like mah-jongg and crossword puzzles. Most discouraging was the failure to convince even the country's intellectuals, or even to get them to understand what humanism was. At the Cleveland Modern Language Conference in December 1929 a semblance of a debate on humanism had taken place, a farce which may have led Babbitt to participate in the Carnegie Hall affair. As one of the humanists, Odell Shepard, tells it, the representative of so-called "humanism" was "a Nicaraguan refugee" maliciously set up as a straw man for the linguist and literary critic. The so-called humanist "sang and gurgled and cooed cadenzas in the best manner of a third-rate Lamartine, descanting upon Soul and Beauty—with at least two capital Bs—until every person in the room with the slightest tincture of decency in him said to himself: 'If this be humanism, then I am not taking any.' "[49]

Babbitt tried to represent the creed properly in his own debate, but if the most educated literature teachers in the country were so easily taken in, what chance did he have with the common man? Shepard hoped that "Sheep may be made to take the right path as easily as to take the wrong." But he was wrong about these sheep and this path.

The Modern Language debate was apparently just another confusion of humanism with humanitarianism. But there were other misrepresentations of humanism that probably kept many potentially sympathetic persons from even reading the works of Babbitt and his followers. In *The Modern Temper* (1929) Joseph Wood Krutch movingly expressed the despair many moderns felt with their loss of faith in any absolute. Yet in an absurd misreading of the humanists he stated that the inner check was best represented by animals who mate only in season, and he put forward the obsessive sexuality of Don Juan as a "characteristically human" act.[50]

In the same year as *Humanism and America* twelve southerners issued their own manifesto, *I'll Take My Stand*. Unlike Krutch, these men—among them Allen Tate, John Crowe Ransom, and Robert Penn Warren—agreed with Babbitt in principle that a truly human life must be rooted in a traditional culture. Still, they assaulted their natural allies as a bunch of ivory-tower academics. The only "genuine humanism" this country had known was not "an abstract moral 'check' derived from the classics"; it had flourished in the old agrarian South and had been "deeply founded in the way of life itself—in its tables, chairs, portraits, festivals, laws, marriage customs." This attack touches upon a weakness in humanism even Babbitt recognized—its lack of immediate unifying symbols. But the agrarians too were guilty of misreading. They accused the humanists of narrow aesthetic interests, of not being "critical enough to question the social and economic life which is their ground."[51] This criticism was only a half-truth. Like most conservatives, the humanists defended property, sometimes capitalism itself. But as for Babbitt at least, anyone who had read *Democracy and Leadership* or even *Literature and the American College* could not fairly accuse him of defending the status quo.

If even America's intellectuals could not agree on what the word *humanism* denoted, why should people suffering from the country's greatest economic crisis be concerned? After 1930, public discussion of humanism dropped off rapidly. The Depression insured that American intellectuals would look to the Left for solutions to America's problems, and the rise of fascism ensured that freedom, not restraint, would continue to be the American ideal. By the mid-1930s Babbitt and More were both dead. By 1942 when America was caught up in yet another great war, the furor raised by the humanist controversy echoed only faintly. Looking back in that year, Alfred Kazin was bemused by the whole business and announced that Babbitt and More "seem fated to be remembered by smaller and smaller groups of academic admirers, and may yet go down merely as the twin elder saints of the old school."[52]

Chapter Four
Humanist Literary Theory

As a literary critic, Babbitt ran quickly into a fierce opposition difficult to comprehend now that new critical theories appear as often as new novels. The opposition was largely a product of academic politics. Departments of English, fairly recently formed and struggling to justify their existence,[1] looked unfavorably upon any critic who valued classical more than postclassical literature. Moreover, English departments were under pressure because the emerging elective system allowed students untrained in the prevailing philological criticism to avoid literature courses.[2] Under such circumstances a critical theory such as Babbitt's that requires extensive learning in Western and Eastern literature was impracticable. In addition, after the 1929 stock market crash the national political climate shifted hard to the left, and Babbitt's political philosophy was hardly congenial to the new social democracy.

Although most of the attacks on Babbitt's theories during his lifetime came from Marxists, socialists, expressionists, and impressionists—as well as from the equally beleaguered philologists and historical scholars, who nevertheless constituted the majority of English professors—the situation clearly favored the new formalist criticism. It was highly teachable to unlearned students, since they had only to focus on one piece of literature at a time without respect to the historical forces that produced it. More important, it claimed a privileged status for literature, distinguishing it from other subjects, thus justifying the expense of hiring specialists in that subject. Best of all, however, it claimed political neutrality, much like science, and therefore seemed much safer and more flexible than the politically charged New Humanism.

Although it took root much earlier, the formalist movement became popular in Chicago in the 1930s under the powerful direction of Ronald S. Crane. His influential essay "History Versus Criticism in the University Study of Literature," published in the *English Journal* in 1935, directly attacked historical scholarship but dismissed humanism briefly.[3] Shortly after Crane's slight of the humanists, John Crowe Ransom's "Criticism Inc." in the *World's Body* called for professionalism and referred to humanism as a brief "diversion" from historical studies, one apparently not to be taken seriously alongside the "more scientific" critical instruments of the new formalism.[4] By 1957, W.K. Wimsatt and Cleanth Brooks, in their two-volume *Literary Criticism: A Short History,* felt justified in giving Babbitt only brief mention in passing and in a few footnotes. To them, Babbitt's criticism was "the all but fanatical result of a theory of literature that was not in fact literary."[5]

Ironically, Wimsatt and Brooks cite T. S. Eliot, Babbitt's most famous student, to support their opinion that Babbitt is not truly a critic of literature. In fact, however, Eliot lay somewhere between the humanists and the formalists. Although he believed that literature should be appreciated as literature, that is, for its formal unity, he remained too much Babbitt's student to divide literary from nonliterary issues. The only danger in not separating these issues, Eliot said in 1929, is that the critic "may lose his detachment and submerge his sensibility." But Eliot unhesitatingly affirmed that "there is no literary problem which does not lead us irresistibly to large problems."[6] But by 1957, the "professional" critics had apparently managed to resist. As far as Wimsatt and Brooks were concerned, humanism with its large problems met its "approximate end" in 1930.[7]

The economic and political conditions of Babbitt's time, both in and out of academia, may explain why the voice heard in so many of his essays seems convinced that the philistines will not understand a word. There is a pathos in these passages, for clearly Babbitt misread the popular trends, directing most of his polemics toward the dryness of the philologists and the airiness of the "present impressionistic-expressionistic imbroglio," and hardly mentioning the newly emerging formalists. In fact, he supported any corrective focus on formal considerations, not guessing that the extreme formalism would prove to be humanism's most dangerous enemy. Today hindsight reveals the theoretical and political cul-de-sac into which the new formalism drove literary criticism. New Humanism would have never encouraged the world to believe that literature was irrelevant to its concerns.

The Notion of Literature

Formalist and humanist critics differ chiefly in their understandings of what literature is. For the new formalists, a poem or a short story is essentially different from a critical essay or a historical account of a battle. The poem or short story is an isolated, discrete object, self-contained to the extent that, though the historical "background" of its production may aid in understanding the meaning of its terms, the "literariness" or "artisticness" of the literary object is entirely separate from that background. "Literature" works according to a unique set of rules, and though, say, a history text may be judged "as if" it were "literature," what it has to say about historical events has nothing to do with its literariness.

For Babbitt, such an easy separation of form from substance—or what amounts to the same thing, such a reification of discourse into a static object suitable for a purely internal analysis—is unthinkable. He clearly does not expect anyone to make such a move in his own age. Of course, he occasionally chides the neoclassicists for attending too strictly to mere form. This tendency he attributes to their "indolent" reliance on models, for he considered such copying a perversion of the doctrine of imitation. As we shall see shortly, he also sharply criticizes Kant's notion of purposeless purpose as an unhappy product of a metaphysical error. But his disdain for any philosophy that sets up art as an end in itself is most clearly demonstrated when he dismisses the most recent manifestation of this error: "The doctrine of *l'art pour l'art* professed by a Baudelaire or a Leconte de Lisle . . . stands in fairly close relationship to the revolutionary fiasco of 1848 (*O*, 172). Babbitt clearly believes that history necessarily influences poetic activity and that critics should not treat poetry as a unique phenomenon divorced from the rest of life. At the same time, however, he believes that art is no mere reaction to historical pressures, unless it lacks, as the art-for-art's-sake movement did, a positive direction: "However one may account for this doctrine historically, the practical upshot of it has been a failure to find any ethical center on which its partial aims and activities finally converge" (*O*, 172).

This last statement reflects Babbitt's distinction between "inner" and "outer" form, a distinction which would have precluded his sanctioning the formalist critical theories of the 1930s and 1940s. This distinction is primarily between forms of purpose and forms of technique. Inner form, or "form in the human sense," Babbitt defines as "the imposition on the raw material of experience of some pattern that has been apprehended with the aid of the imagination" (*O*, 150). At the risk of confusing Babbitt's notion with that of later myth critics, we can say that "inner form" entails a conformity of sense to an archetypal form or vision of what human life means or ought to mean. Whereas for most myth critics, such as Northrop Frye, an archetype is purely an imaginary construction, for Babbitt an "inner form" necessarily places demands on the will. As such it guides or should guide the application of every possible "outer form"—poems, plays, novels, newspaper reports, scientific treatises, sculpture, architecture, music, clothing, furniture—in fact, all forms of human activity.

Thus, although Babbitt believes that intelligibility requires sharp distinctions among the various genres or technical forms of human making, he also believes that the truly great creations of an epoch converge in their inner form. A lyric might be an excellent lyric qua lyric, but fail miserably to achieve inner form. Such a piece Babbitt often will consider "partial" or "aimless." On such grounds, although he praises it for its formal unity, Babbitt condemns Coleridge's "Rime of the Ancient Mariner," since it is not "concerned with moral choices in their bearing on the only problem that finally matters,— . . . man's happiness or misery." Conversely, he may consider a piece that fails technically to be more significant than another, more technically perfect, piece simply by exemplifying, though imperfectly, a "higher" genre. Babbitt recognizes a hierarchy of genres since some kinds of writing are technically more capable of expressing inner form or a more comprehensive representation of human nature: "One must insist that in the house of art are many mansions. It does not follow that all the mansions are all on the same level or of equal architectural dignity" (O, 118). Without question, an epic has a better chance of achieving greatness than a scientific article.

Too often Babbitt neglects to remind his readers that his criticism takes place on two levels. When he says in The New Laokoon that "true art consists in having something to say and then saying it simply" (NL, 230), he reflects his adherence to the Aristotelian concept of art as techne, of the efficient use of materials to achieve a particular end. By this definition making a hydraulic pump is as artistic an endeavor as painting a portrait. Here Babbitt is at the level of outer form. But in "On Being Creative," when he denies "creative" literature its privileged position over criticism, he is at the level of inner form. "Literature" that merely expresses an author's unique personality, his emotions, or some bizarre, fantasized situation, is far less significant than a critical work that subordinates its author's feelings to some higher, more central goal. Criticism can share with poetry and other forms of literature in the narrow sense the highest form of creativity: "the task, especially difficult under existing circumstances, of creating standards" (*O, 26*). The critic shares with the artist the task of achieving "coordinating principles of unity" (26), though of course this task is performed using different techniques on different materials, and though the novelist may have better tools at his disposal for achieving it than the critical essayist. Like the philosopher, the critic confronts "the same central problem" as the artist: "For, to inquire whether the critic can judge, and if so by what standards, is only a form of the more general inquiry whether the philosopher can discover any unifying principle to oppose to mere flux and relativity" (*M,* viii –ix).

Because what is typically called literature has more flexible techniques than the discursive techniques of criticism and the like, it is more capable of being creative, in both the false and the true senses, than criticism. Nevertheless, "one should remember that an even more fundamental distinction than that between criticism and creation is that between good and bad literature. Good literature may be defined as literature which combines excellence of form with soundness of substance" (*O, 23*). Although this appears on the surface much like the formalist distinction between form and content or even more like formalism's latter-day claim that form is content in literature, what Babbitt means here is quite different. Contemporary readers of his work must always bear in mind that his criticism always operates at the level of discourse and not at the "aesthetic" level. The dialectical opposite of form in Babbitt's work is always "expression," not content, and "form" then refers to generic conventions, to the units of discourse that are the common property of those who share a language, while "expressions" are the individual's usage of those conventions in a particular instance. The "soundness of substance" that must be combined with "excellence of form" to achieve good literature is therefore a phrase implying Babbitt's belief that literature is always subject not only to aesthetic but also to ethical judgment. Literature must be made well and made for a worthwhile purpose.

This belief is stated perhaps most memorably in "On Being Creative," an essay written largely in response to J. E. Spingarn's *Creative Criticism.* Spingarn had quoted Goethe as saying that the critic should always ask these two questions: "What has the writer proposed to himself to do? and how far has he succeeded in carrying out his own plan?" (*O*, 28). Babbitt is incredulous: "A man is said to have succeeded in carving images of the twelve apostles on a single cherry stone. A living German is reported to have constructed a perfect model of Cologne Cathedral out of two million and a half match sticks. The critic is apparently confined to congratulating such persons or those who undertake the literary equivalent on their success in accomplishing what they set out to do" (*O*, 28). Disbelieving that Goethe would promote something so foolish, Babbitt finds that Spingarn has neglected to quote Goethe's third question: "Was the author's plan reasonable and sensible?"[8] Babbitt then exclaims, "Mr. Spingarn owes the public an explanation of how he came to reduce Goethe's three questions to two, with the result of transforming him from an Aristotelian humanist into Crocean aesthete" (*O*, 29).

By asking Goethe's third question, humanism simultaneously displaces "literature" from any privileged, isolated position above other writing and places it firmly among writings relevant to history and to the human condition. From "the point of view of inner form which requires imaginative allegiance to some central norm or scale of values set above any particular art" (*O*, 175), all literature, indeed all forms of making, are to be judged by the same norm. Babbitt thus asserts the equivalent of the Marxists' "mediation"—a process which in Babbitt's version integrates the genres. Such integration allows the comparison of texts across generic borders. However, at the level of outer form genres work independently. Attention to generic conventions is a matter of decorum and necessary for the sake of intelligibility. Blurring the boundaries between arts—what Babbitt calls the *mélange des genres*—necessarily lessens intelligibility and heightens the merely idiosyncratic.

Despite the fact, however, that all genres can be judged by the same standards at one level and remain equally distinct and independent at another, there is, as mentioned earlier, a hierarchy of genres based on their capacity to achieve inner form. In this sense Babbitt does recognize a "great literature," tending to use this designation generically for those works best expressing the "idea that must underlie . . . all creative efforts in either art or literature—the idea of beauty" (*NL*, 217).

The Idea of Beauty

If the primary difference between literature in the narrow sense—poetry and the like—and other writing is that it aims first at beauty, then it follows that the kind of beauty an artist aims at is the initial ground of criticism. "Roughly speaking," Babbitt says in "Schiller as Aesthetic Theorist," "one's notions of beauty will tend to vary according as one's total attitude towards life is naturalistic, humanistic, or religious" (*O*, 179). In the same essay he states that "the most widely accepted idea about beauty is that it arises from the achievement of unity in variety" (*O*, 177). The essay as a whole is a Socratic dialectical analysis of the ways in which philosophers, with Schiller as a special focus, have differed in their conceptions of how this unity should be achieved. In short, for Babbitt the problem of beauty is a special case of the more general philosophical problem of the One and the Many.

Accordingly, Babbitt confronts here the same modern error he confronts elsewhere: the tendency to collapse the crucial distinction between human nature and physical nature. Briefly, his argument is that unless one wishes to fall into a rationalistic dryness, best represented by the German *Aufklärer*, he must assume that the unity of a beautiful object cannot be the unit of a determinate concept; it must be an immediate intuition of unity in variety which cannot be reduced to a series of rational choices. Modern philosophy, in Babbitt's view, has created a false dilemma by reducing the possible sources of this intuition to two: the human being's own physical nature (the "feelings" or "aesthetic sensibility") or divine inspiration. In the first case, judgments of taste are relative to the physical, emotional characteristics of individuals and therefore ultimately meaningless; in the second, judgments must be absolute and completely outside all forces of history. Babbitt does not deny either possibility and, in fact, he cites several examples of the former throughout his work. He does deny, however, the relevance of these two kinds of beauty, especially the first, to the human situation.

In Babbitt's view, Kant's *Critique of Aesthetic Judgment* provided the theoretical framework for later concepts of beauty more thoroughly sensationalist than his ultimately rationalistic one. That framework included a sharp separation between reason and imagination which resulted in Kant's claim, abhorrent to Babbitt, that

"As a phenomenon among other phenomena man may . . . be strictly determined and at the same time in the noumenal realm be perfectly free!" (*O*, 144). This doctrine in effect says that the freedom to choose bears no immediate relationship to the capacity to act. The corollary to this doctrine is Kant's assertion that although aesthetic judgments are universal, they are a priori, having no relation to prior experience or practical judgment. More important, since the higher will—in Kant the "categorical imperative"—is thoroughly abstract, not directly intuitable, the cooperation between the imagination and the reason that Kant describes as the function of the aesthetic judgment can be nothing but an illusion. In other words, Kant's aesthetic theory entails a severe contradiction: it seeks to prove "that judgment in art, in spite of the fact that it rests on the taste of the individual and, so far as immediate perception is concerned, does not get beyond the phenomenal world and its infinite otherwiseness, may nevertheless have universal validity" (*O*, 147–48).

This contradiction opens up Kant's fundamentally rationalist theory of art to the sensationalist interpretations it will receive in the nineteenth century, especially as the romantics appropriated his concept of genius. Since Kant can see no access to the higher will, and since the only possible constraint remaining for art is the practical will, Kant conceives creative activity in terms of the free play of the imagination: "It appears to follow that a man has genius only in so far as his imagination is not subordinated to any end, only in so far as it is allowed to play freely" (*O*, 147). In Babbitt's view, Kant's notion of purposiveness without purpose (*Zweckmässigkeit ohne Zweck*) is only a "metaphysical subtlety" which in no way deters the "genius" from indulging merely in his eccentric sensations.

In fact, Babbitt believes, this is the direction (or rather the directionlessness) followed by the entire German romantic movement. Schiller was the first to eliminate from Kant's notion of play its remaining vestiges of purpose. Art became a striving for the infinite, an endless escape from every possible curtailment of desire. Schiller sums up his doctrine when he says that the Greeks "freed the eternally blessed gods from the bonds of every aim, every duty and every care, and made idleness (*Müssiggang*) and indifference the envied lot of the divine estate: a purely human name for the freest and most exalted being" (*O*, 152). Babbitt acknowledges that "Schiller, like Kant, utters warnings against mere anarchy of the imagination" (*O*, 152, n. 1), but charges that neither offers any real constraint for the imagination except for the inadequate discipline of technique.

Since even patterns of unconstrained play produce conventions, the very limitations the romantic genius seeks to escape, artists in the nineteenth century began to pursue novelty for its own sake. In *Rousseau and Romanticism* Babbitt attributes that pursuit partly to a "transfer of the belief that the latest thing is the best—a belief that is approximately true of automobiles—from the material order to an entirely different realm" (*R*, 64). But whether conceived as the absurd but logical conclusion of a false philosophical doctrine or as merely a psychological transference, the practical result of the tendency is the same: traditional norms come to be displaced by undisciplined impulses. Lost in the search for originality, Babbitt complains, is taste, which "involves a difficult mediation between the element of uniqueness in both critic and creator and that which is representative and human" (*R*, 65).

Babbitt's practical criticism reveals his taste to be rather narrow. In his excellent article of 1941, "Irving Babbitt: A Reappraisal," Wylie Sypher asserts that "Babbitt as a critic of conduct appealed to the data of consciousness, whereas Babbitt the critic of literature appealed to formulas."[9] In 1977 J. David Hoeveler will echo Sypher's appraisal, saying that, like Paul Elmer More, Babbitt "tried too much to contain art in a formula."[10] Without doubt, Babbitt's idea of beauty, derived almost exclusively from the art of the Grecian Golden Age, leaves little room for even the most significant art produced in the last two centuries.

From the vantage point of the late twentieth century, Babbitt does seem to be extraordinarily blind to the worth of modern literature. Thomas R. Nevin has noted Babbitt's own "acute awareness of his defensive and solitary position" against most contemporary literature and his conscious, though ineffective, attempts to avoid appearing reactionary.[11] Nevertheless, Nevin finds Babbitt's critical opinions "implacably dour and negative" and observes his aesthetic arguments to display a "strange lack of contemporaneousness."[12] Nevin's review of Babbitt's pronouncements against contemporary American novelists—Dreiser, Norris, Sinclair, Dos Passos—does seem to justify his conclusion that "Babbitt's harsh verdicts on modern fiction were a function of his stringently held classical bias."[13] He seems, in other words, to violate his own contention that a critic "should base his judgment on the widest comprehension and sympathy" (O, 29) and should "have formulae and categories, but hold them fluidly" (NL, 190).

As Nevin has observed, Babbitt faults modern art on two points—its form and its expression. The form of the novel, especially, tended, if not to "formlessness," at least to a "triumph of diffuseness over concentration" (NL, 204). Babbitt's generalization, however, is precipitous, one born out of ignorance. His library, Nevin notes, contained no twentieth-century novels but Aldous Huxley's. Perhaps more telling, nowhere in his published work does Babbitt mention the contemporary novelist most attentive to form, Henry James.

Although it is difficult to accept Babbitt's point about the novel's form, his point about expression is more substantial. Here he offers two major complaints. First, most contemporary literature offers readers only a temporary escape from boredom. This, he says, is certainly not new with the twentieth century: "The need of escape is deep-seated and universal and has been satisfied in manners manifold in the literature of the past" (O, 111). The "literature of the tired businessman" offers only the flight of fancy and no serious challenge to action, no real call to examine the shallowness of one's life. Babbitt rightly dismissed such "literature" as being unworthy of his criticism. The second complaint, directed toward the serious art of his time, is not that literature offers a cheap escape, but that it offers no escape whatsoever.

Commenting on *An American Tragedy*, Babbitt contends that Theodore Dreiser "has succeeded in producing in this work something genuinely harrowing; but one is harrowed to no purpose" (O, 216). Naturalistic literature like Dreiser's arouses "a feeling of sheer oppression" by revealing the enormity of the forces binding the human spirit, but it offers no means for the will to overcome them. Dreiser was not alone in this fault: "Fatalism of the naturalistic type is responsible in large measure for the atmosphere of futility and frustration that hangs heavily over so much contemporary writing" (O, 217).

This condemnation of fatalism saves Babbitt from being a naive reactionary—especially since he even more roundly condemns the romantic art that preceded the naturalistic and realistic. Here he shows his criticism to be progressive, as he says it is. One need only observe the difference between Norris, Dreiser, and London, and later writers such as Percy, Cheever, Hawkes, and Barth, to affirm that the second half of the twentieth century has gone beyond the fatalistic vision of the first. Whether the indifferent, naturalistic world is depicted as an insane asylum (Percy's *Lancelot*), a prison (Cheever's *Falconer*), a bestormed malevolent island (Hawke's *Second Skin*), or a beleaguered ship (Barth's *Sabbatical*), the doomed protagonists have some way out, some form of grace, however gratuitous, however fantastic.

With some justification, many of Babbitt's contemporaries assumed that decorum was the central issue with him when it came to the novel. Dreiser, for example, considered Babbitt of a "toast and tea crowd" who "do not know any too much of Life" and who "would have us carving and polishing amethyst adjectives wherewith to express decorus and not too coarse thoughts. Oh, strike me pink!"[14] Nevertheless, Babbitt likely would have appreciated that these postmodern works transcend the dirt and blood and turn the naturalistic forces to the service of a higher will. Babbitt's quarrel was not with sex and violence in art, but with the proposition that sex and violence sufficiently define the human condition. As he says in *On Being Creative*, "For the interest that may arise from the portrayal of the conflict between a law of the spirit and a law of the members, the inordinate interest in sex for its own sake promoted by most of the so-called realists is a rather shabby substitute" (*O*, 217–18).

As a second point in defense of Babbitt's taste, he in fact does see worth even in the authors he most despises. Even Rousseau "is a great writer and not merely an improviser of genius."[15] And present-day readers should not forget that Babbitt saw a special role for the critic: like everyone else, he is incapable of stepping outside his own historical situation and should not pretend otherwise. "The humanist critic," he affirms, "does not cultivate exclusively either the truth or the counter-truth but mediates between them; only, according to the special conditions with which he has to deal, he may lean to one side or the other" (*O*, 29). Since Babbitt saw himself living in an era that had taken Rousseauian romanticism to its very extreme, he believed his duty as a critic was to oppose that tendency extremely. A comment on Goethe's criticism reveals that he is well aware that his criticism may appear dogmatic: "Goethe leaned very strongly to the side of comprehension and sympathy as a corrective to the dogmatic narrowness of many of the critics of his time. The present emergency is the exact opposite of the one that confronted

Goethe. Open-mindedness is being glorified in the critic as an end in itself" (O, 29–30).

If Babbitt were writing today and his practice consistent with his theory, his criticism would be weighted in an opposite direction. Consider the ultraformalism of poststructural criticism and literature, the displacement of human and civil rights issues by New Right politics, the pro-corporate bias of supply-side economics, the antihumanism of "Moral Majority" fundamentalist religion, the formulaic "audience-tested" plots in cinema, the mechanical rhythms of minimalist and popular music, and the "back to basics" movement in education. These all indicate an extreme shift away from the glorification of the spontaneous individual that culminated in the 1960s. But if the present trend toward cultural standardization continues, the result could make the neoclassicism of the eighteenth century seem like a veritable orgy of sympathy and creativity.

The function of the critic, however, is not merely to counter the prevailing trends. An originality that merely inverts the extreme values of its predecessors is mechanical; it avoids the difficult labor of forging human norms suitable to a unique present without invalidating the past. In order to achieve this goal, Babbitt repeats tirelessly, "one should aim first of all not to be original, but to be human, and . . . to be human one needs to look up to a sound model and imitate it" (R, 64).

The Doctrine of Imitation

Artistic imitation transforms imaginative play into imaginative work. The goal of that work Babbitt describes in a variety of terms: the illusion of a "higher reality," the creation of universal human standards, the presentation of representative fiction, to name a few. His concept of imitation is quite possibly more subject to misinterpretation than his other central concepts, since the term's everyday usage implies that, contrary to Aristotle's meaning of it, that which is imitated has form prior to its being imitated. When something has received prior formations, Babbitt refers to the process as the imitation of models. Such secondary imitation is not necessarily an error. "Many of the neo-classics," he says in "On Being Creative," "show that this type of imitation is compatible with genuine creation" (O, 14), although secondary imitation always risks falling into "mere copyism" (O, 15). However, Babbitt is more concerned with promoting imitation in the primary sense, a sense very close to Aristotle's, which is "not only flexible and progressive, but in its own way, positive and experimental" (*R*, 36).

Babbitt claims that "Aristotle bends his whole effort to showing that imitation may be ideal, or, as we should say, creative" (*O*, 11–12). Whereas Kant's "genius," or the faculty of imaginative play, is incompatible with imitation, Aristotle's imitation provides a focus for play, converting the aimlessness of mere play into the purposiveness of genuine work. The work is not ordinary, of course, not the everyday, situation-specific, often alienated work of pragmatic life. It is work best conceived as the task of giving intelligible form to the structures that underlie human activity.

These structures appear remarkably similar to Fredric Jameson's Marxist description of the symbolic as a resolution of "determinate contradictions" of desire located in a prior historical "subtext, it being always understood that 'subtext' is not immediately present as such, not some common-sense external reality, not even the conventional narratives of history manuals, but rather must itself always be (re)constructed after the fact."[16] There is a vast difference, certainly, between the Marxists' view of history, in which the social body progressively alters over time until all such contradictions are resolved, and Babbitt's view that only the individual's understanding of his or her place in the historical flux can progress. Babbitt's criticism of Sainte-Beuve's organic view of history applies equally to the Marxists' progressive view: "Sainte-Beuve was perhaps too much haunted by this notion of the classic age,—the notion that a country like an individual has its period of childhood, and adolescence and full maturity and senile decay. This is another 'biological analogy' that I for one distrust profoundly. If we must have a theory, the theory of the saving remnant might be more to our purpose than that of the classic age" (*NL*, 240). In other words, for Babbitt the general situation of history is always the same— always a tendency toward an extremist monism producing false dichotomies. As these tendencies shift from one extreme to the other, history moves like a pendulum, back and forth. History displays no growth, as in cyclical histories, no progression, no regression. Certainly, the world is always changing, but the task of the humanist "saint" never changes: he must recover the balance of the opposing forces which are the underlying reality of history.

For example, imitation and imagination are the opposing forces

whose resolution comprise the creativity problem. Babbitt resolves
them abstractly by asserting that imitation "becomes creative in
direct proportion as it succeeds in rendering the universal through
the particular" (O, 12). The problem can be resolved really, of course,
only though concrete ethical actions, fictional or factual. Creative
representations of a universal truth of human nature must at the
same time imitate prior representations of the same truth. In this
sense John Barth's *Giles Goat Boy* is a conscious secondary imitation
of *Oedipus Rex,* although anyone who has read both works must
concede that copyism is out of the question because Barth's resolution of the conflict between the individual and communal selves
takes a form peculiar to twentieth-century America, just as Sophocles' resolution takes a form peculiar to fourth-century B. C. Athens.

Another difference between Babbitt's and the Marxists' understanding of the historical "subtext" lies in the way each conceives
its effectiveness. For the Marxists, the "determinate contradictions"
of the subtext, which are unconscious and not under the individual's
control, mark the limits of the individual's possibilities for conscious
action, and thus the function of symbolic activity is to resolve these
contradictions, negating their effectiveness. Babbitt's understanding
is precisely opposite: so long as the passions are unformed they are
random, directionless, and thus ineffective. The function of imaginative imitation, then, is to control these forces by submitting
them to a consciously chosen inner form, one of "universal" human
norms, thus giving the emotions purposeful direction and giving
the individual a sense of the unity of his desires with those of others.
Although certainly the outer formation of desires—anything produced by man—will differ immensely from culture to culture, period to period, work to work, and individual to individual, great
literature reveals that the inner formation of desires may be nearly
universal.

Accordingly, Babbitt asserts that Aristotle's concept of catharsis
"can be interpreted rightly only in the light of his doctrine of the
universal. A great tragedy portrays passion and portrays it vividly;
at the same time it generalizes it. The spectator who is thus lifted
into the atmosphere of the universal tends to be purged of everything
that is petty and purely personal in his own emotions" (O, 12–13).
Catharsis in this sense is quite different from the psychoanalytic
appropriation of the term "to describe the relief one gets by ex-

pressing oneself freely" (*O*, 18), or perhaps more accurately by disseminating libidinal energy. Babbitt says that H. L. Mencken reveals his false conception of catharsis when he claims that the critic "is first and last simply trying to express himself. . . . He is trying to achieve . . . for his own inner ego the grateful feeling of a function performed, a tension relieved, a *katharsis* attained which Wagner achieved when he wrote *Die Walküre* and a hen achieves every time she lays an egg" (*O*, 18–19).

The difference between Aristotelian and Freudian catharsis, like the difference between Babbitt's imitation and Marx's production, is an instance of the more general difference between the teleological and the genetic methods. Teleologically, things are partial manifestations of an emerging totality; genetically, things are products of an existing totality. Babbitt makes his position quite clear in his introduction to *On Being Creative* when he discusses the book's epigraph from Aristotle: "The first is not the seed but the perfect" (*O*, xi, n. 1). To use the genetic method—to discuss the man-made thing in the same way one would discuss a natural object, to discuss human activity in the same way one would discuss a biological process—is to commit a basic error in category application. Natural processes are entirely positive; human activity is fundamentally negative. Human beings have the capability to negate, to refuse to act upon impulses. The imitation of an imaginatively grasped "sound model of human nature" gives the individual both purpose (to realize positively the model) and direction (to negate systematically the impulses that conflict with that purpose). Clearly, creative imitation thoroughly resists genetic explanation.

However, just as clearly, human beings seldom, if ever, act entirely according to the discipline and vision required by creative imitation. Socrates, Aristotle, Confucius, Buddha, Jesus—such men may have had original visions of human nature, but even these visions are subject to criticism, not only because of occasional inconsistencies, but also because human nature, being just as complex and its elements even more subject to transformation than those of physical nature, will inevitably prove the model to be incomplete. This fact, however, is really beside the point as far as Babbitt is concerned, since truly human living lies in the struggle to achieve a "centrality of vision" and in the inner peace that accompanies it. The individual must struggle to wrest a balance from conflicting impulses, both physical and cultural. In every historical period conflicting models of human nature overlap and interpenetrate every region of human activity, fragmenting experience.

A person living today, for example, may have his understanding of an ordinary circumstance affected by the competing claims of Christian dogma, behavioral science, capitalist economics, socialist humanitarianism, Freudian psychoanalysis, existential philosophy, and other regional models of human nature. Such a person may consciously imitate a model in one area of life but forget or ignore it in another, but most of his actions will be less than conscious, the product of habit or the subconscious transference of past patterns upon the present. Certainly, fragmentation of this kind should be expected of the ordinary person since even the works and especially the lives of great authors reveal the conflicts, contradictions, and inconsistencies of adhering to a necessarily partial imitative model, even when that model is followed with the strictest discipline.

Babbitt's doctrine of creative imitation carries important political, philosophical, and critical implications. Politically, the extraordinarily wide range of imitative completeness that an individual may achieve, from the politically alienated neurotic extremist to the religious (not necessarily theist) prophet, when combined with his belief that no one can ever achieve the Truth, provides a foundation for Babbitt's highly elitist conception of constitutional democracy, best summed up by his suggestion that democracy "substitute the doctrine of the right man for the doctrine of the rights of man" (*DL,* 246).

Philosophically, the doctrine eliminates the possibility of an unconscious. It is certainly the case that individuals often act impulsively, not consciously according to a norm but according to structures of which the individual may be unconscious; but that does not mean that there is an unconscious. The higher will, the very capability of human beings to refrain from impulse, negates all views of a total structure inaccessible to consciousness that determines and therefore accounts for rational action. According to Babbitt, Freudian psychoanalysis develops "what may be true of the hysterical degenerate into a complete view of life" (*R,* 262).

But if the imaginative constructs that reflect inner form are neither conscious transformations of prior imitative models, nor gifts of divine inspiration, nor the products of unconscious processes, psychological, political, or otherwise, then where do they come from?

His answer, as chapter 2 indicated, is grace. Finally, grace means only that the search for the ultimate origins of such forms will always end in mystery. Although at first glance such an answer may appear to reveal a fatal flaw in Babbitt's philosophy, to him it simply indicates that the vital question to ask of an imaginative construct such as a work of art is not "Is it true?" in the absolute sense but rather "Does it work?" Can it provide norms for human action appropriate to its historical situation without negating the norms of the past?

Babbitt's grace represents the ultimate limits of the human will. On the one hand, humans are incapable of achieving a total explanation of the material ground of behavior through rational means; on the other, they are incapable of grasping a totalizing construct of human nature understood as purposefulness through imaginative means. Simply put, human life cannot be adequately understood as either actuality or illusion. The great error of the neoclassicists, according to Babbitt, was their claim that judgment was superior to and different from the imagination. The romantics retained this opposition but elevated imagination over reason. "If there is to be any important advance in criticism at the present time," says Babbitt, "a first step would seem to be to overcome the neo-classic and romantic opposition between reason and imagination and seek to recover the Aristotelian idea of a cooperation between the two" (*O*, 93).

Babbitt locates the idea in Aristotle's injunction to "imitate things not as they are but as they ought to be" (*NL*, 9). Human "reality" lies in the concrete, particular, genetically explainable behavior of individuals which is the subject of history, but its significance lies in the illusion of purpose which is revealed only in fiction, myth, plot. If the artist "should give us truth, but a selected truth, raised above all that is local and accidental, purged of all that is abnormal and eccentric, so as to be in the highest sense representative" (*NL*, 10), the critic should continue that same work by finely discriminating among the elements that constitute literary works, comparing these elements over the broadest possible range of literary history, developing as a result of this comparative, dialectical analysis a set of critical standards which are those "patterns of normal experience" that have come to represent "the constant factors in human nature itself" (*O*, 142–43). It must be remembered, however, that for Babbitt "human nature" is not composed of a given set of opinions or inclinations; rather, it is the product of the relationship between the material ground of positive existence and the purely human capacity to refuse to act upon the inclinations that that ground produces.

Genre Criticism

Humanism's unrelenting emphasis on the will to refrain has tended to raise the voices of those who do not read Babbitt closely enough and find only rules, nothing to rule. Harry Salpeter's 1930 essay "Irving Babbitt; Calvinist" represents the worst of these unfounded reactions: "Babbitt's Humanism is compounded of fears, timidities, denials, rejections. It is more dogma than Humanism. It is the rationalization of a thinness of emotion, a lack of impulse, an incuriosity, if not hostility, to all flowerings of the human spirit . . . . Never having had the impulse which required the operation of restraint, men like Babbitt would like to impose a law of restraint upon men more richly endowed."[17]

Such remarks tell us much more about Salpeter, truly more about the crude state of the American academic institutions that sanctioned ad hominem arguments by publishing them, than they tell us about Babbitt's thought. However, they do tell us something of the historical situation in which Babbitt's thought took place, for Salpeter's unrestrained emotion in a critical essay exemplifies what Babbitt believed was a rapidly spreading disease in Western civilization— an "expansive" emotionalism, and its chief symptom, the *mélange des genres*, confusions of literary categories.

Genres are the products both of a kind of inner logic and of a convention, understood in its literal sense of a group of people coming together and agreeing to do a thing in a certain way. The way may not be the only way to do a thing, but it may be the best way to achieve a certain purpose given certain circumstances. Greek tragedy, for example, was formed by the standard or conventional laws of representing the universal paradox of identity. Here Babbitt means by law "the establishing of a causal sequence between a number of certain isolated facts or phenomena," and of course he means "the facts of human nature" and not those of physical nature (*NL,* 202).

Because "the genres are related not merely to the natural law, but in a vastly higher degree to the 'law for man' " (*NL,* 215), literary genres work quite differently from natural classes. Babbitt agrees with Diderot's naturalistic claim that "Everything is a perpetual flux; every animal is more or less man; . . . every plant is more or less mineral; there is nothing precise in nature" (*NL,* 215). However, Babbitt quickly warns against what he calls the biological analogy: "Because the genera and species evolve and run together in this way on the physical plane, it is easy to take the next step and assume that the literary *genres* evolve and run together in the same way" (*NL,* 215).

The difference, though simple, is profound. Whereas natural genera evolve randomly by filling an environmental niche, literary genres evolve, or rather develop, toward an imaginatively grasped purpose through conscious selection. Since human nature never changes, in one sense literary genres can achieve perfection: they can develop to a point where development is no longer necessary. This is why Babbitt agrees with Aristotle when he says that "Tragedy after passing through many transformations finally found its true nature and there it stopped" (*NL,* 215–16). Nevertheless, there is a sense in which genres necessarily change. Babbitt emphasizes this sense when recommending that contemporary artists look to the ancient Greeks: "The actual forms in which the Greek embodied his mediation between extremes are relative and need not be literally revived; but though relative, as particular forms must always be, they point the way to laws that are absolute" (*NL,* 250).

In other words, Babbitt recognizes a distinction similar to Northrop Frye's between modes and genres. In *Anatomy of Criticism* Frye begins his essay on the theory of modes by noting, "In the second paragraph of the *Poetics* Aristotle speaks of the differences in works of fiction which are caused by the different elevations of the characters in them. In some fictions, he says, the characters are better than we are, in others worse, in still others on the same level."[18] Since, Frye says, "the importance Aristotle assigns to goodness and badness seems to indicate a somewhat narrowly moralistic view of literature," Frye will determine his own fictional modes "not morally, but by the hero's power of action, which may be greater than ours, less, or roughly the same."[19] Accordingly, Frye reduces the fictional modes to five—the mythic, the romantic, the high mimetic, the low mimetic, and the ironic. Genres, however, represent an author's "intention of producing a specific kind of verbal structure"[20] in a particular social situation. Thus "the genre is determined by the conditions established between the poet and his public."[21] As Fredric Jameson has pointed out, Frye's modes (which Jameson calls the semantic or phenomenological approach to genre) are defined in terms of dialectical opposites—comedy as opposed to tragedy, or to irony. Genres (which Jameson terms the syntactic or structural approach), however, are opposed only by their simple negation—the opposite of comedy is simply not comical.[22]

Babbitt's genres are similar to Frye's modes, and what Babbitt calls the "actual form" of genres is similar to Frye's genres proper. Although Babbitt's theory is certainly not as systematic as Frye's, it is clearly Frye's nearest predecessor, but one that fully retains Aristotle's moralistic sense of generic difference.[23] Of course, Frye's and Babbitt's categories are not exactly parallel, since Frye makes distinctions according to the hero's power to act, whereas Babbitt makes his according to motives for action. For example, Frye's distinction between the "tragic" and the "comic" is "a general distinction between fictions in which the hero becomes isolated from his society, and fictions in which he is incorporated into it."[24] Babbitt's distinction between the romantic and the classic is similar, except that the romanticist longs to distinguish himself from the community whereas the classicist strives to represent it. Similarly, just as Frye's modes can combine to produce, say, tragic irony or ironic comedy, Babbitt's romanticism and classicism have their ironic modes (see chapter 2). In Frye these combined modes are morally neutral. "The central principle of tragic irony," for instance, "is that whatever exceptional happens to the hero should be causally out of line with his character."[25] In Babbitt, however, as we have seen, romantic irony reveals a failure to apprehend a moral distinction between the human and nonhuman.

In *The New Laokoon,* his full-length discussion of generic differences, Babbitt notes only in passing that genre (in the second sense of actual form) is governed by "the boundaries that are imposed on each art by its own special technique, the material in which it works, its relations to time and space, etc." (*NL,* 233, n. 1). He adds, "I am of course approaching the subject from an entirely different angle." For Babbitt, the "actual form" is the locus of the shaping, constraining, concentrating forces of genre and the "vital," expressive, spontaneous eruptions of the concrete and particular from the historical flux. Unfortunately, he never discusses explicitly the relationship between genre, in his sense, and its actual form, despite the fact that this relationship is crucial to his theory.

Since *The New Laokoon* focuses primarily on genre rather than form, Babbitt has been taken to be more formalistic than he actually is. However, thinking spontaneity generally ran uncontrolled in his own time, in his practical criticism he does indeed emphasize the "shapely" over the "vital," leaving himself open to attacks such as Salpeter's. Babbitt warns against leaning too heavily to balance an imbalance, "for extremes are barbarous, and if an artist lean too one-sidedly toward either the shapely or the vital, he is in danger of ceasing to be humane" (*NL,* 232). Not only artists but also critics can fall prey to this danger. Babbitt sharply reproaches Lessing for "tending to disassociate language from emotion, to allow insufficiently for the unconscious and the spontaneous, in short, to treat art too analytically" (*NL,* 52). Ironically, his own criticism is, at least from today's point of vantage, subject to the same reproach.

However, Babbitt was battling what he considered a fundamental category error, the confusion of expressionism with expression, sometimes stated as a confusion between "the spontaneity of instinct and . . . that of insight" (*NL,* 224). Those who would argue that spontaneous, instinctive responses to the world prevent the deadening effects of traditional categories presuppose a fundamental split between a self that thinks and a world that is thought about. Romantics, especially, presuppose a "natural," reliable reality and an artificial and therefore suspicious intellect. When the relationship between the self and the world is conceived this way, it follows that our only reliable responses to the world are our own natural—that is bodily, emotional—responses.

For Babbitt, reliance on impulse or instinct is an illegitimate, nonhuman reaction to the continual problem of the inadequacy of categories. His belief that an individual can avoid the tyranny of traditional categories thinly separates his philosophy from that of his German contemporary, Martin Heidegger. Heidegger believed that the self is always already in the cultural world, that the self can have no grasp of nature "as it is" but can think, perceive, feel that which is not the self only through the cultural formations of the tradition into which the self is born. He taught that to achieve an understanding of oneself one had to "listen," to respond quietly to the tradition, to allow its projects to become one's "own." Like

Heidegger, Babbitt believed that the significance of the world lies entirely within the tradition; and like Heidegger, he believed that the tools for understanding the tradition (in Babbitt's term, genres)—and thus the self, since these are the categories with which one knows oneself—can come from nowhere but the tradition. But Babbitt's recommended attitude toward the tradition is hardly that of passive receptiveness.

To the contrary, his attitude is one of aggressive conservatism. It is conservative because he believed that the tradition, understood as the clearest expression of unchanging human nature, offers the only means to understand one's common or representative self, the very foundation of civilization. His attitude is aggressive because Babbitt equally believed that it required tremendous effort to resist perceiving the tradition one-sidedly and partially, to avoid elevating a circumstantial truth to an absolute, when the only truth men can know absolutely is that they cannot grasp the absolute truth. Since the humanist aims to wrest the freedom of individual decision from cultural determination, he must be a critic whose task is to disclose and condemn those claims of universality that can be only partial.

In order to accomplish this task, the critic must be able to compare the various incarnations of a truth claim over a long period, since only collective experience can separate the representative from the peculiar expressions of human nature. So criticism must be genre criticism. The actual forms of historical genres, with their particular designs for specific purposes, must be preserved—their differences must be preserved—so that they can be compared. Although at first such a doctrine seems to be a merely dry conservatism, the product of a museum curator's mentality, the upshot of the doctrine is quite radical. Babbitt holds that unless specific generic differences are held intact, the specific locality and limitedness of particular works cannot be discerned, and if not discernible, the historical changes within genres cannot confirm the sameness of human motivation beneath the historical differences.

It would seem, then, that *mélange des genres,* the confusion of categories, would present an insoluble interpretive problem for a critic like Babbitt, but it does not. It is an irritation but not a problem. In fact, Babbitt recognizes no true interpretive problems. If one believes in a universal human nature—balanced and opposing drives represented by standards (or genres) which are never fully formulated but only approximated in differing circumstances—then quite obviously the problem is not understanding the local genre but grasping the universal norms. When the critic applies these norms consistently across the entire tradition, no matter what these norms may be, the individual works and their local genres will always differ consistently. Individual works do not reveal the universality of human nature: universal norms reveal the locality of individual works.

Certainly, great literature represents universal norms in particular situations. Still, a major task of criticism is to prevent such particulars from being taken as truly universal. To accomplish this task, the critic must have access to these norms in advance of any critical activity, even if the critic must "create" those norms or standards. The critic's norms must be derived from the past, although they may be modified by life experience, and they must conform to the law of measure—for measure permits deliberation, choice, and truly human judgment.

Thus Babbitt's understanding of generic criticism resembles that of E. D. Hirsch, who believes that interpretation moves from broader to narrower categorizations of a text until one grasps its "intrinsic genre," a construction of the author's final purpose or intention. However, Babbitt's first concern is not for what an author meant to say within the context of his own situation, but for what an author is actually saying within the context of the critic's present and as it is grasped within the structures of the critic's standards. Only from this point of view can local and relative intentions be discerned.

Conclusion

In the memorial essay "A Portrait of Irving Babbitt," Austin Warren notes that "Babbitt's mind set early into its permanent position,"[26] that his basic attitudes and standards never altered but only became more encompassing as his attention shifted from particular works of French literature to the most general issues of Western and Eastern thought. As Warren hints, Babbitt's opposition to his father's transcendental and humanitarian philosophy partially explains the early achievement of his "integrated and inflexible intellect." Whatever the genetic cause, Warren says, Babbitt "seems, indeed, to have been born full grown."[27] From a theoretical point of view, the Babbitt we know could not have been "born" any other way: his brand of criticism requires a fully developed set of standards already in place.

But if Babbitt's opinions on works, movements, language, and culture changed little, his capacity to reflect on the meaning of those opinions developed greatly. His first books (editions of French works published in his late thirties) show little theoretical awareness, but beginning with *Literature and the American College* (1908) he becomes increasingly theoretical and reflective. Yet he never seems to recognize that the essence of his philosophy is a thoroughgoing skepticism. As early as 1912, in his chapter on Renan in *The Masters of Modern French Criticism*, Babbitt seems to come close when he accuses Renan of false skepticism. According to Renan, " 'the blaming of this or the praising of that is the mark of a narrow method' " and criticism should entail the " 'excluding of all exclusiveness' "(*M*, 259), an attitude Babbitt thinks is typical of modern criticism. Babbitt's point is that Renan merely shifts the authority for judgment from the standards of the individual critic to the "objective" criteria of positivist science.

Babbitt's own praise and blame represent a much more thorough skepticism, for the path of humanism is a narrow one between a multitude of opposing errors, leading not to the infinity of heaven but to the finite righteousness of being merely not wrong.

Chapter Five

Humanism and the Psychology of Education and Politics

For Babbitt, education, cultural history, politics, and religion were too interrelated to treat separately. In the opening paragraph of *Democracy and Leadership* he wrote that "When studied with any degree of thoroughness, the economic problem will be found to run into the political problem, the political problem in turn into the philosophical problem, and the philosophical problem itself to be almost indissolubly bound up at last with the religious problem."

In practice, however, Babbitt treated all these as psychological problems. He attributed social ills to a breakdown in the inner life, to the loss of an equivalent for grace, and sought to convince individual men and women to convert themselves to life under the law of measure. If enough individuals underwent conversion, directly experienced the psychological truths the humanist sages taught, America could again be a just republic. Above all, he believed, the country needed conversion of its leaders so they might serve as models setting the ethical tone of the state. Lacking an aristocracy from which to draw its leaders, America must create one by means of education for character and wisdom. Unless it could do so, it would be ruled by plutocrats and demagogues and someday might require a man on horseback to save it from the mob.

Humanism and Education

Literature and the American College appeared in 1908, the last full year in the administration of Harvard's President Charles William Eliot. The timing was probably not coincidental. For four decades Eliot had played a central role in transforming the small American college with its traditional classical curriculum into the modern

American research university with its endless variety of courses and degrees.

Eliot aimed at curing some real evils in a higher education no longer relevant to American life. The Puritans founded Harvard, America's first college, to create a learned aristocracy that would keep their city on a hill from degenerating into barbarism. When President Urian Oakes addressed the graduates of 1677 as *liberi liberaliter educati* (gentlemen, educated like gentlemen), he conferred duties as well as privileges; the Puritan gentleman was expected to be at once a saint, a philosopher, and a statesman. But American conditions quickly eroded this medieval ideal. By the mid-nineteenth century, hundreds of colleges like the College of Montana had sprung up across the nation—"pathetic, libraryless little boardinghouses for drillmasters" Richard Hofstadter calls them. Every new town wanted to become a new Athens, and each religious sect wanted its own college. Yet the colleges, even Harvard, were hardly centers of intellectual ferment; their primary purpose was to inculcate morality and to supply "mental discipline." Most students were poorly prepared and spent most of their time memorizing elementary lessons to be recited daily in class. Graduate work was a different matter, however. Requiring only three years' nonresident study and a pro forma oral examination, the A.M. degree meant, as a current saying put it, little more than "keeping out of jail five years and paying five dollars."[1] After the Civil War colleges realized they would have to adapt to a rapidly industrializing society. In 1869 Harvard turned to Eliot, an M.I.T. chemistry professor who, as the title of his recent *Atlantic Monthly* article phrased it, had converted to "The New Education."

Both a Rousseauist valuing his students' uniqueness and a Baconian devoted to scientific progress, Eliot had, in Babbitt's view, irreparably harmed American education by instituting the elective system and by encouraging original research in all academic fields. Although Babbitt himself had fled the regimented, intellectually sterile College of Montana, he still could not approve Harvard's excessive liberality and progressive spirit. In *Literature and the American College,* the fruit of more than twenty years' experience with the elective system and the new university, he repudiated virtually everything Eliot had achieved. Nevertheless, he knew a return to the past was impossible. He could hope only to correct the worst abuses of the new education while saving what was best in the old.

The new education: Rousseauist dream and Baconian nightmare. Siding with Rousseau against the doctrine of innate depravity, Eliot established his free elective system so that each Harvard undergraduate could follow his "spontaneous inclinations, natural preferences, and easiest habitual activities."[2] By 1897, Harvard students faced only freshmen rhetoric as an obstacle to their absolute freedom to choose. In addition, they could graduate with Cs in one quarter of their courses and Ds in the rest. Harvard may have been the hardest school to get into, but it was also the easiest to stay in.[3] The elective system's self-evident absurdity called only for Babbitt's satiric restatement: "The wisdom of all the ages is to be as naught compared with the inclination of a sophomore. Any check that is put on this inclination is an unjustifiable constraint, not to say an intolerable tyranny." Failing to understand human nature, Eliot thought students would joyously pursue their own interests but instead merely enabled them "to lounge through their college course along the line of least resistance."[4]

On his Baconian side, Eliot emulated the German university's commitment to scientific method and original research for graduate students. In 1872 he established the Graduate Department (which later became the Graduate School of Arts and Sciences). By the 1890s, many major universities were hiring Ph.D.'s exclusively, and Harvard had become a leader in turning them out. Babbitt was all for rigor in graduate study, but he believed students should achieve the intellectual breadth and balance that lead to wisdom. The specialist, he thought, was likely to become "a poor lop-sided fragment . . . built into the very walls of the Temple of Progress" (44). The philologists were worst of all; having an "incapacity for ideas" (133) themselves, they forced their graduate students to crank out dissertations on trivial subjects before developing sound critical standards.

He also feared that the faculty would lose the old ideal of academic leisure. This was an age when Frederick W. Taylor, the apostle of scientific management, conducted efficiency studies on college faculties to make sure they were not wasting time. Leisure for contemplating and assimilating ancient wisdom was giving way before the "perpetual devil's sabbath of whirling machinery" (262). Lacking "the idea of repose," the university, like the society it mirrored, looked on teachers and students as instruments "for the attainment of certain outer ends" and set up "the worship of energy and mechanical efficiency" (251). Babbitt believed in having definite ends, but the highest of these was a fully human life, which no amount of scientific progress could produce.

The greatest evil to Babbitt was that specialization, perhaps not entirely improper for graduate study, was invading the college (the term then designating only the undergraduate school). In 1890 Eliot had merged the Lawrence Scientific School with the college, blurring the distinction between the A.B. and S.B., the latter having been a three-year degree for less-qualified students. He was willing to let many students loaf through school so long as some could advance quickly to their fields' frontiers and begin specialized research. Although he failed to reduce the traditional four-year undergraduate curriculum to three years, he persuaded the college to grant credit for high scores on entrance examinations. By 1906, some thirty-six percent of Harvard's hustling students were graduating in three years anyway. In addition, advanced undergraduates could take graduate courses, a practice that further undermined the college's integrity.

Behind these reforms lay Eliot's humanitarianism. From the elementary grades on, he wrote, students must learn "that the desire to be of great public service is the highest of all ambitions." As long as a student developed his "power" to solve problems, the subject didn't matter. Needless to say, classical study failed to meet this criterion. Eliot professed no antipathy toward the classics themselves, but the elective system destroyed the old hierarchy of studies, creating a Darwinian struggle within the curriculum. "In education, as elsewhere," Eliot announced, "it is the fittest that survives. The Classics, like other studies, must stand on their own merits. . . ."[5]

Others more directly attacked the college and the old curriculum. Hugo Munsterberg, a Harvard philosophy professor, argued that since there were only two kinds of scholars—"receptive" and "productive" (*LC,* 100)—the American three-tiered system of high school, college, and graduate school did not correspond to psychological realities. He would eliminate the college and institute the German system of gymnasium and university. Furthermore, he depreciated traditional scholarship as "passive" and "feminine" (101), a charge guaranteed to raise Babbitt's hackles. One of Babbitt's greatest concerns, in fact, was that Munsterberg's criticism had an element of truth, for philologists weren't the only teachers undermining the old ideal.

The others were the "dilettantes," whom Babbitt associated with the "feminine" Rousseauist spirit. He saw in the modern university what Ann Douglas has seen in the larger culture—the feminization of a disestablished group. In Douglas's interpretation of nineteenth-century American culture, men, especially businessmen, seized control of practical life and relegated ministers and women to the passive, "feminine" role of supplying a spiritual "influence" on the virile male when he wasn't hustling for money.[6] In Babbitt's view the hustling Baconian philologists had relegated many literature teachers to a similar role; untrained in *strengwissenschaftliche Methode,* such teachers could justify their places in the new university only on the grounds that literature provided spiritual "uplift." Babbitt noted with alarm the large coeducational universities of the Midwest, where men flocked into the science courses while women filled the "sissy" literature courses. He could already see the day "when the typical teacher of literature will be some young dilettante who will interpret Keats and Shelley to a class of girls" (119).

Dilettantism threatened even all-male Harvard. As Babbitt saw it, modern Baconians exhausted by their strenuous endeavors turned to literature as a mild, soothing narcotic. (For Babbitt, a Baconian was anyone—scientist or businessman—whose standard of value was efficiency.) He no doubt had in mind the hundreds who flocked to hear Charles Townsend Copeland, the famous "Copey," read publicly in his beautifully modulated voice or to hear Barrett Wendell follow his soulful classroom poetry readings with cries of "Isn't it beautiful?"[7] Such Baconians suffered a pyschic split reflecting "the masculine and the feminine aspects of the same naturalistic movement" (128). Without an infusion of the humanist spirit, literature instruction would be divided between the "masculine" philologists and "feminine" dilettantes and would cease to be the source of "a law of life" (119).

The humanist alternative: "All the space between."   Babbitt often turned his opponents' arguments against them. For example, he emphasized the "positive and critical" basis of humanism to counter the scientists' claims to authority. He refuted Eliot's Darwinian argument much the same way. True, he admitted, disciplines must prove their fitness, but the classics already had—through "the selection of time" (82). Over the centuries experience had separated the essential from the inessential to create educational standards. Each man, however, assumed selection in an environment that suited his argument. For Eliot, it was the shifting spontaneous inclinations of undergraduates; for Babbitt, an enduring normal human nature. Until that changes, he implies, colleges had better not embrace the new.

Babbitt was but one of many who defended the traditional curriculum, but, following Pascal's dictum to harmonize opposite virtues and "occupy all the space between them" (22), he hoped to occupy the middle ground between extremes. The reactionary extreme had been represented in the previous generation by Yale's President Noah Porter, though many of Babbitt's older contemporaries, including Charles Eliot Norton, defended "liberal culture" on similar grounds. Porter's was the traditional argument for mental discipline: because the classics are so difficult to learn, they are a kind of mental gymnastics whose effects are "inwrought and ingrained into the very structure of the intellectual and active powers." At the other extreme was the dilettantish Cornell English professor Hiram Corson, who argued that "wise passiveness" in attuning oneself to the "informing life" of each literary work would create "soul states" influencing the reader's "unconscious personality." Corson, like many others, clearly identified the weaknesses of scientism and vocationalism but gave only the haziest notion of the culture he defended. The period was, in Laurence R. Veysey's phrase, "the great age of moral homily." Lacking a scientific methodology, educators were forced into vague generalizations, like those of President Merrill Gates of Amherst: "The mission of the college is to diffuse the beneficent light of ideas. . . . The pressing want of our time . . . is manly men, of liberal culture and sound head and heart, in every walk of life."[8]

In the earliest-written essay in *Literature and the American College*—"The Rational Study of the Classics" (1897)—Babbitt can match Gates moral homily for moral homily: "The classical spirit, in its purest form, feels itself consecrated to the service of a high, impersonal reason" (174). Babbitt recognized, however, that the age's muddled impressionism required correction. His extended definition of humanism, constituting the book's first two chapters, gives his argument the substantial philosophical basis his contemporaries' arguments lacked. The book also reveals a great concern with the active intellectual life. Babbitt acknowledged that literature exerts a subconscious influence (in the Arnoldian sense of forming character), yet he was hostile to dilettantes who read literature for "mere titillations of the aesthetic sensibility" (115). He wanted Porter's discipline and Corson's attention to the informing life of individual works for a purpose those men did not recognize: a "vigorous and virile application of ideas to life" (133). He believed studying the classics would link students with their own tradition and thus relieve them of the vague sense that their lives "may be deficient in depth and dignity" (167). It would also teach them to value the Greeks' "creative imitation"—the delicate balance "between the forces of tradition and the claims of originality" (135). Finally, it would give them a feeling for "form and proportion, good taste, measure and restraint, judgment and discriminating selection" (136). But even if all of this were true, Babbitt realized, he still needed to counter Munsterberg's contention that America's traditional educational system failed to reflect psychological reality.

Munsterberg recognized only receptive and productive scholars— the extremes; Babbitt mediated between these extremes, asserting a middle stage of psychological development when humanist education was necessary. College-aged students, he wrote, have become "capable of reflection. This change from the receptive to the reflective and assimilative attitude of mind is everything from the humane point of view, and contains in fact the justification of the college" (100–101). Babbitt chose his terms carefully. "To reflect" (literally to "bend back") suggests the humanist's discrimination and judgment. "To assimilate" is to "make the same" and suggests the humanist's ability both to identify those few enduring ideas in the world's great literature and to make those ideas part of his or her own nature.

To distinguish humanistic learning from "feminine" dilettantism and to avoid charges of sterile attachment to the past, Babbitt insisted that reflection is a task "virile above all others" and that the assimilation of the best that has been said and thought, "so far from lacking in originality, calls for something akin to creation" (101). The teacher assumes a priestly role in a sacramental act: "The ambition of the true college teacher is not to 'distribute' knowledge to his students, not 'to lodge it with them,' as Montaigne says, 'but to marry it to them and make it a part of their very minds and souls' " (102). The college years thus become a necessary gestation period before ideas emerge fully developed in legitimate scholarly productions. Munsterberg's "productive" scholars, not married to knowledge, could produce only bastard offspring.

In his heart Babbitt probably wished to restore a prescribed classical curriculum, but he realized that the Baconians and Rousseauists would not go away. The true humanist, he was forced to argue, does not turn his back on the present: "His aim is not to deny his age, but to complete it" (259). An age that trains only for Eliot's "power and service," that believes in efficiency and sympathy but lacks moral standards and fails to balance sympathy with selection, is clearly incomplete. It produces the "philanthropic brigand"—a Rockefeller or a Harriman. These men are models of efficiency and sincerely desire to serve, "Yet a few more Harrimans and we are undone" (68). America could not protect itself from such men by attacking capitalism as a Rousseauist would; it must induce its future Harrimans and Rockefellers "to get themselves rightly educated" (71). If such men could become complete human beings, the country could avoid fluctuating between extremes.

Harvard, Babbitt saw, tremendously influenced American culture. Harvard's liberal reforms had been emulated by most other American colleges; he hoped humanistic reforms would have the same result. Perhaps then the university could once again help conserve rather than disrupt the traditional order. Before the Civil War Harvard had been a great stabilizing force. As one historian puts it, "For the domineering yet anxious elite, the cultural constellation [centered in Harvard] served as conservative traditionalism served other countries—as a 'center,' so to speak, 'that would hold.' "9 Unfortunately, the New England bankers, shipping magnates, and mill owners who sent their sons to Harvard, married their daughters to Harvard graduates and professors, and endowed chairs in the sciences and practical disciplines gradually imposed their values on the college (forty percent of Harvard graduates were entering business by the mid-1890s). Like the rest of the country, Harvard was beginning to feel "the full impact of a brutal naturalism" (63) that could be counteracted only if an aristocracy educated for character and wisdom replaced the aristocracy of money.

Having felt Charles Eliot Norton's influence, Babbitt was certain the example of a few educated, virtuous men could change the country's ethical tone. However, his belief in aristocratic influence conflicted with another—the Aristotelian belief that government should reflect the ethos of the governed. Reformers argued that the new university was simply responding to the practical, democratic, progressive spirit of America; he would later counter that the true American ethos was Puritanism, the humanist "saving remnant" serving the exemplary role of the Puritan "visible saints." But he offered no concrete plan for restructuring the college or society. He was a philosopher and critic, not a social engineer. Nevertheless, he had one very practical suggestion for balancing the curriculum: the addition of A.B. and A.M. degrees granted with distinction. In 1907 Harvard had indeed taken a step back from the free elective system by instituting an honors A.B. With the further addition of an honors A.M., Babbitt believed, the humanist would have a place in higher education, as long as the degree required the assimilation of ancient and modern literatures and not original research. Such a degree would avoid dilettantism and narrowness while still demanding a "solid discipline in facts" (142). What's more, it would train literature teachers, something the Ph.D. failed to do.

If such a degree program were implemented, the problem would still remain how the Rockefellers and Harrimans would become rightly educated. Such men would certainly avoid the A.B. with honors, devoting themselves to practical studies and seeking the dilettantes for spiritual uplift. Babbitt's plan could ensure the saving remnant's survival (perhaps that's all he hoped for), but it could never make humanistic ideas the warp and woof of the social fabric.

Eliot's successor, Abbott Lawrence Lowell, moved against the elective system's excesses by introducing majors and minors, thus ensuring that each student knew "a little of everything and something well." He also encouraged the honors A.B., so that by the 1930s about forty percent of Harvard's students graduated with honors. These reforms, however, merely compromised between the hustlers and dilettantes. Although forced to get a smattering of general culture, many students plunged so deeply into their specialities that by 1936 the official Harvard historian was boasting of undergraduate honors dissertations worthy of Ph.D. students at the turn of the century.[10]

As late as 1930 Babbitt was promoting a graduate degree requiring assimilative reading instead of original research, but his plan was soundly defeated. In these last years he also began promising his followers a book on "Humanism and Education," meant to be the capstone of his thought and a practical program for hu-

manistic education. Finally, however, he could discover no way to
order the chaos of American education. The manuscript fragment
in the Babbitt Papers at Harvard is largely a nostalgic view of
humanist education from ancient Greece to the Renaissance and
breaks off at the moment Rousseau turned childhood into an ideal
instead of a state to outgrow. When Babbitt described Erasmus
struggling to uphold a lost ideal of "symmetry" in the midst of the
Reformation, he was doubtless expressing his own feelings: "The
sense of his growing isolation amid the various . . . irreconcilables
cast a shadow upon all his later years."

The irreconcilables darkening Babbitt's own last years were largely
the ideals of "service" and "power" that Eliot had preached during
the reformation of the American college and that had been carried
forward by John Dewey and other liberal theorists. In 1929 Babbitt
surveyed American life and enumerated the rotten fruits of Eliot's
training for service and power: a "Rotarian Convention" covering
commercialism with a veneer of idealism, a "drift toward standard-
ized mediocrity" due to the loss of standards, hustling college professors and students who resembled nothing so much as "the tired
businessman," and a lust for power promising future horrors like
the Great War.[11] America obviously had not found a way to get its
Rockefellers and Harrimans rightly educated.

Humanism and Politics

Although he freely denounced his contemporaries' Progressive
programs, Babbitt offered no specific political program himself. He
was a "philosophical" conservative basing his theory of government
on man's dualistic nature and drawing upon the wisdom of Greece
and Asia, the stolid British conservatism of Edmund Burke, and
America's own "great unionist tradition" (*DL,* 273) extending back
through Lincoln to Washington, Marshall, and Adams.[12] Like the
Progressives, he recognized that laissez-faire capitalism had produced a brand of rapacious individualism leading to monstrous inequalities; unlike the Progressives, he wanted to convert America's
leaders rather than extend democracy or arbitrarily redistribute
wealth. Fearing the tyrannical rule of the majority, he intended
Democracy and Leadership as his contribution to "a specific problem—
to the distinction, namely, between a sound and an unsound individualism" (*DL,* 317). The "experiments" of history revealed that

states led by sound individualists who restrained their desires achieved the essential virtue of civilization—justice; states led by unsound indvidualists who gave free reign to their impulses quickly degenerated into barbarism.

America, Babbitt believed, was yielding to the seductive humanitarian schemes of unethical leaders, schemes masking a lust for power and domination and leading to injustice, internal strife, and imperialistic aggression. Babbitt was not sure mankind could escape the forces pushing it towards Armageddon. As a result, *Democracy and Leadership* expresses an unresolved tension between his hopes and fears—between his belief that men and women are free moral agents and his suspicion that human nature is a biological trap, between his dream of a civilized state that rewards virtue and his nightmare of a Hobbesian world of *bellum omnium contra omnes,* the universal war of all against all.

Leadership and the just state.   Like Plato and Aristotle, Babbitt saw an analogy between the just individual and the just state. The just individual's higher self coordinates and controls the "inferior parts"; the just state is "only a reflection of the harmony and proportionateness" achieved by just leaders (*DL*, 198). The most obvious implication here is that the state, like the individual, has a lower, inferior element needing restraint. Pursuing this analogy, the Greeks, including Aristotle, had justified slavery as a natural consequence of the slaves' animality. Babbitt faulted Aristotle for inadequately appreciating freedom, yet, as will appear below, some such division of mankind lies behind his own darker prophecies. However, making it central to his political theory would have forced him to accept an authoritarian state incompatible with individualism. His ideal state would have very few laws and external controls; it therefore presupposed a citizenry with at least a modicum of the imagination and *frein vital* necessary for a human, civilized life.

Babbitt's assertion that justice in the state is a "reflection" of justice in the leader links his politcs with his aesthetics—with one important difference. Whereas the artist freely chooses his model, most people, it seems, imitate their leaders instinctively. For Babbitt, the "most encouraging trait" of human nature is that people are "sensitive to a right example. It is hard, indeed, to set bounds to the persuasiveness of a right example, provided only it be right enough" (*DL*, 308–9).

Collateral testimony from Aristotle, Confucius, Christ, and Buddha supported this theory. Aristotle had argued that the man of character is the measure of all things; however, he erred in identifying character with reason, for reason had led the Greeks into skepticism and intellectual pride and had not long sustained their civilization. Babbitt thus resolved "to put Confucius behind Aristotle and Buddha behind Christ" (273). Confucius recognized that "the ultimate root of character is humility" (35) and that will is necessary to the law of measure. Yet Confucianism always threatened to stiffen into rigid formalism, and Christianity, which also recognized the need for humility, was tied to an authority "anterior, exterior, and superior" (175) to the individual. The sound individualist must be self-reliant as well as humble, a combination Babbitt saw most of all in Buddha, a "thoroughgoing individualist" (170) who found standards without sacrificing the positive and critical spirit. Somewhat like the artist who keeps his eye on the human norm in creating works of primary imitation, Buddha recognized the higher will as the unifying principle in human nature and embodied it in his own conduct, thus making himself available for secondary imitation. Like Christ, he became "the Word . . . made flesh" (171).

If enough sound, humble individualists could become leaders, a sort of ethical trickle-down would bind society. For Babbitt, humility was not self-abasement incompatible with the gentleman's *sprezzatura;* it was simply the recognition that one has not met a high standard. The person who "look[s] up to something higher than . . . himself" becomes "worthy to be looked up to in turn" (*DL*, 200), and so on down to the bottom of the social hierarchy. Though this seems a fanciful notion, Babbitt saw its workability illustrated in Confucian China, whose stability for two millenia he attributed to Confucius's own exemplary character and insistence on ethical leadership. Here was evidence that man might after all be "a reasonable animal" (34).

Besides possessing humility, the leader must work to close the gap between his own flawed nature and the standard or model— whether a superior individual or an imaginatively conceived human norm. This work always produces character and happiness, but in a just society it will also yield more tangible fruits. For Babbitt, as for Aristotle, justice was the proportionate distribution of property as well as a proper subordination, or, as Babbitt summed it up, "To every man according to his works" (196).

Unfortunately, work had become debased from the moment Francis Bacon, accepting the late scholastic divorce between religious truth and reason, set the intellect free on the natural order. Babbitt traced a "utilitarian movement" extending from Bacon through John Locke, Adam Smith, and David Ricardo to Karl Marx, who all defined work in terms of physical labor. Marx especially took "a purely quantitative view of work" (191), placing a Raphael and a common sign painter on the same level. Sentimental Rousseauists cooperated by idealizing the laborer and stigmatizing other kinds of workers as "hangers-on and parasites" (192) deserving death. This utilitarian-sentimental notion of work had naturally led to the despotism and degrading servitude of Soviet Russia.

Against these leveling, quantitative conceptions, Babbitt argued for a hierarchy ascending from physical, to mental, to "genuinely ethical working" (202)—"the superimposition of the ethical will upon the natural self and its expansive desires" (197). As Buddha recognized, one's work varies as one wishes to be a carpenter, king, or saint: "One simply passes, as one mounts in the scale, from an outer to an inner working" (194). Justice requires that one also mount in the economic and social scales; the "quality of a man's work" should alone "determine his place in the hierarchy" (202) so that the class divisions could be drawn along ethical lines.

Babbitt's aristocracy would avoid the extremes of rigid caste and pure democracy. On the one hand, the "natural aristocrat" (202) with superior abilities would rise through competition. On the other hand, a leisured class existing on inherited property and status would provide stability. In any civilized society some persons must be free from manual labor so they "may engage in the higher forms of working and so qualify for leadership" (203). Leisure does not free one to follow the lower self's dictates—that would be enslavement. "The only true freedom," Babbitt writes, "is freedom to work" (201). Forcing persons of superior mental and spiritual capacities to labor with their hands is tyranny. Property that frees one for ethical work becomes "a genuinely spiritual thing" (272). Babbitt's major quarrel with aristocracies such as the French Old Regime was their treating property as an end rather than a means. Ceasing to be exemplary, the French aristocrats deserved to fall. All Babbitt would ask for any American aristocracy was the punishment of indolent individuals rather than whole classes.

The difficulty here is that competition in America was creating a plutocracy, not an aristocracy. Radical reformers would simply dismantle the system and redistribute the wealth more equitably. Babbitt, however, insisted with Aristotle that "it is not the possessions but the desires of mankind which require to be equalized" (204) and that the only way to do so is by educating individuals to want less.

Babbitt hoped to raise an aristocracy on a democratic foundation—a common basic education for all citizens. Society, he felt, should first transmit its conventions to children in the form of right habits and then provide a common curriculum (literally a "running together") that disciplines them "to some ethical centre" (303), or standard. He did not explain, but he apparently wanted a competitive education that would determine the social hierarchy. Just before denouncing Dewey's corruptions of higher education, he asserts that "The democratic contention that everybody should have a chance is excellent provided it mean that everybody is to have a chance to measure up to high standards" (312). Ideally, it would seem, those consigned to manual labor would have failed to measure up to intellectual and ethical standards, while those assuming leadership in the professions, politics, and business would have first proved their character. Babbitt thus implies an invidious comparison between manual work and ethical work that, as will appear below, helps explain his intolerance of the labor movement.

In Babbitt's just society class conflict and monstrous inequalities would not exist. Workers habituated to want less would not begrudge their bosses' "exceptional rewards" (193), and the bosses themselves would be models of restraint. The problem of giant trusts which so troubled the age would presumably disappear; economic competition, currently "pernicious strife," would become a "sound rivalry" among gentlemen, giving life "zest and savor" (205).

A just society would need few laws; except for ensuring the national defense, the chief executive would have little to execute. Like the Chinese ruler Shun, he could do nothing, yet govern well. "Religiously self-observant," Confucius said of Shun, "he sat gravely on his throne, and that is all" (200). By following Plato's dictum to work first on their own characters, leaders like Shun would indirectly achieve the international peace the reformers' World Courts and Leagues of Nations could not. A state whose leaders are "minding their own business in the Platonic sense" will also mind its own business and serve other states "by setting them a good example" (309).

Finally, however, exemplary humility and ethical work were not enough in a leader. Matthew Arnold had recognized America's need of "a steady exhibition of cool and sane criticism" (281). Babbitt agreed and so determined "to bring Socrates to the support of Christ" (284). Because the average person was easily swayed by abstractions, the historical meanings of general terms must be preserved. All such terms are subject to at least two interpretations; a "Socratic remnant" (281) was thus needed to "dichotomize" them and test the different meanings against the facts of human nature and the historical consequences of accepting one meaning over another. (Babbitt himself dichotomizes frequently in *Democracy and Leadership,* as when he distinguishes between quantitative and qualitative definitions of work.) Socratic leaders would thus prevent the multitude's being persuaded "by a mirage of words that the ship of state was steering a straight course for Eldorado, when it was in reality drifting on a lee shore" (281).

Babbitt's leaders resemble judges more than executives. Babbitt, in fact, considered the Supreme Court the nation's ethical center, "the higher or permanent self of the State" (307). He did not draw neat analogies between human faculties and political institutions, but the Supreme Court seems to combine the *frein vital* and the analytical intellect. It is the veto power on the majority's impulsive will and discriminates by applying a high standard—the higher law expressed by the Constitution. Presumably, the justices are Socratic critics protecting the Constitution's terms from sophistic modern definitions.

In treating American political institutions Babbitt drew heavily on Aristotle and Edmund Burke. Aristotle believed that governments reflect the ethos of the governed; Babbitt believed America's constitutional democracy reflected its historically Puritan ethos. Ignoring the founding fathers' largely deistic, rationalistic temper, as well as the early New England Bible commonwealths' authoritarianism, he simply defined Puritanism as a national *frein vital*: "Puritanism, our national principle of concentration, is the indispensable check on democracy, our national principle of expansion" (252). Although the Puritan theocracy crumbled, its educational system continued to produce men of character, who eventually institutionalized the principle of control in the checks and balances of America's constitutional government. In theory, Babbitt saw a need for the expansive democratic principle, but he insisted that a just state, like a just person, balance expansiveness with concentration, *élan vital* with *frein vital*.

Burke was one of Babbitt's "true liberals," for he recognized that a free government requires its citizens to put duties before rights. Perhaps more important, Burke possessed a "moral imagination"— the ability to see past forms and great leaders as "imaginative symbols" (104) binding the hearts of the nation. "We ought," Burke wrote, "to venerate where we are unable presently to understand" (107). Babbitt lacked Burke's ability to turn a Marie Antoinette into a glorious symbol of the age of chivalry, but he tried to find humanist symbols in America's own past. Above all, Babbitt would have Americans venerate the great "unionists"—Washington, Marshall, and Lincoln. Thus his humanism was not alien to all American traditions as the Southern Agrarians thought, though Babbitt was not poet enough to give his unionist tradition much imaginative appeal.

Babbitt has been called an enemy of democracy, a joyless authoritarian wanting an all-powerful ruling class that would force its arbitrary values on all others.[13] Joy does have little place in his humanistic scheme, and the childhood education he favors could easily lead to regimentation. At times his discussions of the body politic even imply the individual's absorption into an organic state. Yet he hated external authority, insisted on mediating between principles and emergent events, and lauded the founding fathers for not granting sovereignty to any person, class, or institution. Many of his political goals have enormous appeal: a distribution of wealth, power, and privilege according to proven ethical worth; freedom to rise in the social order through superior achievement; a sense of community encouraged by common standards, a shared educational experience, and reverence for a common heritage; and—most important—social order resulting from emulation, not external restraint.

To later philosophical conservatives such as Russell Kirk, Babbitt has seemed the first full flowering of America's conservative spirit.[14] However, difficulties arise when one considers the practicability of Babbitt's ideas. Beyond some vague statements regarding the need for competition, he never offered any means for identifying his men of character, getting them into leadership positions, and justly distributing the nation's wealth without confiscating it. Furthermore, he aimed at the seemingly impossible goal of creating a humanist class, possessing the Puritans' vital control, out of an expansive and humanitarian ethos in order to change that very ethos, even though he recognized that American conditions had created a "frontier psychology" (240).

Compounding these difficulties, he offers little hope for relieving suffering under the existing economic system. The profound changes he desired would take many years, perhaps generations. He occasionally admitted the value of social sympathy, but he most often treated humanism and humanitarianism as equivalents to truth and error that allowed no mediation.

This resistance to humanitarian reform was partly the response of the self-made man who sees others' failures as moral weakness. But it also expressed a deep ambivalence about human nature and the possibility for civilization's survival. In Babbitt's most positive formulations humanism is a philosophy leading to purposeful human action. His aesthetics assume a creative tension between expression and form, *élan vital* and *frein vital*—both are good, both necessary. In theory, even his politics assume the interaction of expansive and contractive principles. Yet most of his pronouncements about contemporary America condemn the expansive principle, aim to stifle change rather than mediate between the old and new, the One and the Many. *Democracy and Leadership* is haunted by the fear that only a few men possess reason and will, that society's lower self is dark and dangerous, that irreversible historical forces are threatening to annihilate mankind.

The squirrel cage of history. Babbitt was absolutely convinced that the higher will existed, but nevertheless recognized strict limitations on it, claiming to have discovered "hard sequences of cause and effect that bind the present inexorably to the past" (*R*, 83). The human law differs from natural law but is every bit as certain: "[T]he person who violates it exposes himself to certain consequences in much the same way that the person [does] who puts his finger into the fire . . . " (*DL*, 234). The person who understands the human law can therefore solve "the only problem that finally matters—the problem of happiness or unhappiness" (234). The human law appears under two aspects—the law of measure and the law of "Nemesis" (Babbitt's term for the principle of retributive justice inherent in the universe, after the Greek goddess of that name). Obeying the one brings happiness; disobeying the other, misery. Unfortunately, most men and women are under the sway of Nemesis. The human proclivity to pursue a dominant desire seemed so universal and the punishment so severe that Babbitt detected "a certain treachery in life itself" (181).

He identified mankind's dominant desires with the three traditional Christian lusts: the lust of knowledge *(libido sciendi)*, the lust of sensation *(libido sentiendi)*, and the lust of power *(libido dominandi)*. Because man is "the infinite animal" (137), a desire neither moderated by the inner check nor mediated by its opposite becomes a boundlessly expansive lust bringing about Nemesis. There was no logical reason this should be so; it was simply an observable cause-and-effect sequence. Babbitt devoted a good part of *Rousseau and Romanticism* to demonstrating the forms of Nemesis visited on the Rousseauist lusting for sensation (spiritual restlessness, suicidal despair, solipsistic isolation), but he believed the greatest threat to civilization came from the *libido dominandi,* a "fundamental will to power" (*R,* 193) that, as history showed, emerged in direct proportion to the relaxation of traditional checks.

Because he believed in the higher will, Babbitt divorced himself from all linear philosophies of history, whether the fatalistic pessimism of Oswald Spengler or the evolutionary optimism of the Social Darwinists and Marxists. Such theories denied the possibility or need of ethical action. But if one were to learn from the past, history must reveal patterns. "The movement of mankind," he argued, "is not steadily forward in a straight line . . . but circular, like that of a squirrel in a cage" (*DL,* 221). The image of a swinging pendulum would have accorded better with his belief that mankind oscillates between extremes; however, both cycles and pendulums suggest repetition without progress. Where, then, does the ethical will come in? Babbitt does not explain, but his point seems to be something like this: As Confucian China and medieval Christian Europe had shown, civilizations can remain reasonably stable for millenia if they have symbols or standards for directing the higher will, and the most powerful standard is the man of character. If, however, those symbols or standards lose their force, if those leaders become unethical, civilization starts on an irresistible descending curve into barbarism. In that "if" alone lies the possibility for creating or preserving a humane world.

Babbitt believed the West was approaching the bottom of what he termed "the imperialistic cycle" (152). As this cycle was revealed in Roman history, "a constitutional republic resting ultimately on religious control gradually gave way . . . to an equalitarian democracy which in turn passed over with the usual incidents of class war into a decadent imperialism" (151). A similar pattern had marked the history of Greece at the time of the Peloponnesian War, ancient China at the time of the Fighting States, and France at the time of the revolution.

The imperialism Babbitt feared most was a "decadent" imperialism; he did not mind conquest so much if the rulers represented a "triumph of character" (162), as he thought the British did in India. Decadent imperialism was characterized by a morally indolent populace and ruthless leaders pursuing their own advantage or that of some class or faction, usually under the guise of noble idealism. Pure democracies lead to imperialism because they destroy the humility and subordination necessary to restrain impulse—*élan vital* becomes the *libido dominandi*. Owing to innate human inequalities, leaders must arise; in a nation without ethical standards they are likely to be imperialistic. Rousseau had posited a disinterested "general will," but Babbitt viewed the notion as "mystical in a bad sense" (90–91). As eighteenth-century France (his paradigm of decadent imperialism) illustrated, the general will was simply the egoistic will of the imperialistic leader writ large.

The French Revolution and the Napoleonic Wars had anticipated the mass slaughter witnessed in the twentieth century. The Great War was both an effect and repetition of the Napoleonic Wars, the "original genius" of the eighteenth century passing through Nietzsche and manifesting itself in German imperialistic Kultur. When the Russians threw off their chains, they merely reenacted the age-old drama; as a current saying put it, "overthrow the Czar and the Bolshevist has you by the throat" (221). Sympathy and reason had once more proven their impotence against the *libido dominandi*. In 1914 millions of European socialists had marched off to slaughter their brothers. And American foundations like the Carnegie Endowment for International Peace had given huge sums so that academicians, among them Babbitt's old antagonist Charles William Eliot, could prove by the "art of comparative statistics" that war is evil. To Babbitt, men who thought war resulted from insufficient data resembled Molière's foolish dancing master, "who held that all the evils of the world arise from not knowing how to dance."[15]

Babbitt even suspected "a sort of synchronism" (*DL,* 131) between pacifistic schemes and war. However invalid this generalization might be, it accurately defined the psychology of many American idealists. Leading Progressives viewed the Spanish-American War and the country's other Latin-American adventures as a noble chance to spread American civilization to supposedly benighted lands. After the turn of the century the monied elite dominated the American peace movement, fearing war would interfere with their economic conquests. When America entered World War I, most Progressives and pacifists ardently supported the crusade to save the world, many joining imperialistic-minded organizations like the League to Enforce Peace. [16]

America had resisted complete democratization and class war— but just barely. Thomas Jefferson and Andrew Jackson had been America's Rousseau and Robespierre, the one preaching a theory of natural rights, the other overthrowing "quality" and asserting the imperialist's "To the victors belong the spoils" (246). The Jeffersonian emphasis on rights had led directly to the Civil War, states' righters and abolitionists constituting "two opposing camps of extremists and fire-eaters" (248) whose dispute had to be settled by force of arms.

Here Babbitt revealed the limitations of his dialectical method. Having placed "rights" in dialectical opposition to "duties," he could not determine whether some rights supersede some duties; his argument gives the impression that a stable social order is all-important, even though it mean some men and women live enslaved. If he intended something else, he ought to have said so, but as often happened his single-minded pursuit of a rhetorical purpose precluded a rounded estimate.

Lincoln had saved the Union from the extremists, but he was the last great unionist. The last vestiges of Puritan restraint were, it seemed, being overwhelmed by an expansive imperialistic democracy. Economic opportunity without ethical standards had encouraged a ruthless scramble for money that made the multimillionaire "the characteristic product of a country dedicated to the proposition that all men are created equal." If these "commercial supermen" didn't have the mass following of a Napoleon, they had exploited their opportunities "in a very Napoleonic fashion" (256).

Babbitt thought America had narrowly escaped a real Napoleon in Woodrow Wilson, the bespectacled ex-college president now popularly considered a democratic saint martyred at the hands of Machiavellian Europeans and power-hungry American politicians. Always suspecting Wilson's idealism, Babbitt was not surprised when America came to the brink of a war for "service" (268) during Wilson's attempt in 1914 to depose Mexico's Victoriano Huerta. Napoleon had made France the "Christ of Nations" (130); Wilson had made America the "Sir Galahad of Nations" (269) on a quest to make the world "safe for democracy." When Wilson took his Fourteen Points directly to the American people, circumventing Congress, Babbitt saw the demagogue's desperate efforts "to make light of the constitutional checks on his authority and to reach out almost automatically for unlimited power" (288).

Wilson's economic policies also seemed a dangerous threat to order. The more conservative Teddy Roosevelt had attacked only particular evil men and corporations; Wilson had tried to regulate competition—openly siding with labor against capital and supporting "class legislation" favoring some groups while taxing others previously favored. He won the very close election of 1916 only by forging alliances with farm and labor blocs, especially in the West. "The whole art and practice of government," Wilson proclaimed, "consists, not in moving individuals, but in moving masses."[17]

For Babbitt, a government concerned with masses threatened individualism and presaged the class war France had experienced during the Terror—a "bucolic episode" demonstrating that "the last stage of sentimentalism is homicidal mania" (126–27). Wilson and many Progressive leaders had become enthralled by "the phantasmagoria of social justice" (298), which threatened to destroy the nation's higher self embodied in its political institutions, especially the judiciary. The Supreme Court had traditionally overturned laws regulating wages or hours as infringements on workers' and employers' freedom of contract. In 1908, however, Louis Brandeis had persuaded the Supreme Court that Oregon's ten-hour law for women was constitutional, thus opening the way for other laws protecting workers' health, safety, and morals. Later Wilson's close advisor and, after 1916, a Supreme Court justice, Brandeis was likely one of the judges Babbitt considered to "have so solicited the strict letter of the law in favor of what they deemed to be socially expedient as to fall into a veritable confusion of the legislative and judicial functions" (296). Right at Harvard Law School, Roscoe Pound had become the leader of a "sociological" school of jurisprudence, asserting that "the judge makes the actual law" by adjusting legal principles to changing social conditions. [18] This seems the kind of mediation between principles and emergent events that Babbitt himself wanted, but when it came to the judiciary, he was a strict interpretationist. Lawyers like Pound were simply "boring from within" (307) to weaken the republic's foundations.

From today's perspective, some of Babbitt's statements on the Progressives' social justice appear irrational: "Social justice . . . means in practice class justice, class justice means class war and class war, if we are to go by all the experience of the past and present, means hell" (308). Historians now generally consider Progressivism a largely conservative, middle-class effort to save America from revolution by correcting the more obvious evils in its political and economic systems. [19] But even fairly innocuous reforms such as the referendum, recall, and popular election of senators impressed Babbitt as symptoms of a vast movement in Western culture toward pure democracy and decadent imperialism.

He perhaps saw truth in Aristotle's contention that revolutions begin with trivial events; however, in fairness, it should be pointed out that many events in Babbitt's day were indeed ominous. *Democracy and Leadership,* though published in 1924, reflects the turbulent postwar years more than the "normalcy" under Harding. In the aftermath of the war many feared the Russian Revolution would sweep the world. In America the years 1919 and 1920 saw attempts by the railroad brotherhoods to nationalize the railroads; the founding of the American Communist Party and the Communist Labor Party; violent strikes by Seattle shipyard workers, the Boston police, steel workers, and miners; a series of bombings, including one that killed or injured over two hundred people on Wall Street; and the great Red Scare with its massive arrests and deportations of supposed Communists. From Babbitt's point of view, such events must have seemed the logical consequence of Wilson's idealistic New Freedom, which, instead of looking to the nation's higher self to restrain the majority's tyrannical impulses, sought social renewal "from below" by "releasing the energy of the country." [20]

High explosives. Babbitt could not console himself with the belief that the pendulum would inevitably reverse its swing. Although he denied progress in human nature, he recognized immense progress in releasing the forces of physical nature. The imperialistic cycle had always produced bloody violence, but only in modern times had man begun to discover means "to blow himself off the planet" (143). Ever since Bacon had projected the ancient dream of a Golden Age into a future utilitarian Utopia, science had been a lust—the *libido sciendi.* Without ethical standards, scientists were already seeking to unleash the power in the atom. The usual argument, also heard before the war, was that no one would dare use the terrible new weapons. Knowing better, Babbitt prophesied that the breakdown of controls would produce the "fools and madmen" (144) certain to use them.

Although modern weapons were dangerous, Babbitt felt that "Under certain conditions, human nature itself may become one of the highest of high explosives" (289). A "moral realist" thus must assert the truths of the inner life in opposition to the "cloud-cuckoo-land" (289) idealists. With the threat of an explosive human nature in the background of his thought, Babbitt's psychological analysis in *Democracy and Leadership* resembles European power politics. In its struggle to maintain "hegemony" (308), the higher will must league with reason and imagination against the lower impulses. Imagination holds the balance of power; if it somehow leagues with a lower impulse, that impulse becomes an infinitely expansive, perhaps explosive, lust.

Some persons, however, struck Babbitt as virtually incapable of self-restraint: "When released from outer control, they are simply unchained temperaments" (*R,* 157). If such temperaments ever constituted a majority, a just state unified by the emulation of ethical leaders would be impossible. The state's *élan vital* would become a national *libido dominandi,* which, if unchecked, would lead to "a triumph of anarchy followed by a triumph of force" (*DL,* 311). Circumstances could indeed arise in which fascism might be the better of two alternatives: "[W]e may esteem ourselves fortunate if we get the American equivalent of a Mussolini . . . to save us from . . . a Lenin" (312). In fact, these circumstances seemed rapidly approaching.

Beginning in the 1880s, millions of dark-complexioned, impoverished immigrants had flooded America from eastern and southern Europe. Many were Catholic or Jewish; some had socialist or anarchist leanings. America's "Anglo-Saxon" elite recoiled from this new foreign element filling the urban slums and creating discontent in the working class. When applied by men of racist leanings, discoveries in genetics suggested that the poverty and vice found among urban immigrants were inherited. Since the "lower" im-migrant races outbred the Anglo-Saxon, "the American type" seemed threatened by extinction. This fear of genetic disaster was preached by such diverse men as Teddy Roosevelt; Lothrop Stoddard, whose pseudoscientific *Rising Tide of Color* caused a sensation in 1920; and even Edward A. Ross, a respected sociologist whose 1914 *The Old World in the New* described the immigrants' "pigsty mode of life," "animal pleasures," and "coarse peasant philosophy of sex."[21]

Babbitt was not a thoroughgoing racist, as evidenced by his reverence for the wisdom of China and India. But he did believe some of his contemporaries' racist theories. Expressing only mild skepticism, he acknowledged the menace in Stoddard's "rising tide of color" (210) and referred to statistics indicating the loss of "qual-ity" in the growing population. Because of sexual license, he wrote, the white race, the "stocks to which the past has looked for its leaders," was lowering its birth rate while "the inferior or even degenerate breeds" were rapidly multiplying (210). According to Harvard psychologist William McDougal, "an observer of the bi-ological type" whom Babbitt cited as authority, America was "speed-ing gaily, with invincible optimism down the road to destruction" (245).

Babbitt's fear of a growing underclass of unchained temperaments does not contradict the antinaturalistic basis of humanism. He thought "spiritual indolence" to be "the most fundamental" (316) trait observable in humanity and believed only "a small minority" (310) capable of more than a rudimentary self-discipline. He denied the universal application of deterministic, naturalistic theories, not their truth to large areas of life. Wilson wanted to release the energies from below; Babbitt wanted to repress them, for the alternative seemed to be a violent release of *libido dominandi*.

This side of his thought probably accounts for much of his op-position to American labor unions. Although he blamed much labor unrest on the "extreme psychic unrestraint" (205) of America's cap-italists, when it came to a conflict between labor and management he quickly sided with the latter on the grounds that management ability represented a superior form of work, ignoring that his theory grants privilege only to ethical workers and that intellect is part of man's natural self. He accused labor unions of undermining stan-dards, citing dramatic decreases in productivity as evidence, and of threatening "partial or total confiscation" (206) of middle-class investors' savings (investors, as Nevin points out, like Irving Babbitt).[22]

Worst of all, labor seemed to threaten constitutional democracy. When Wilson supported the 1916 Adamson Act granting railroad workers an eight-hour day, he yielded to threats of a nationwide strike. Ignoring the workers' grievances, Babbitt called the act "a form of the instinct of domination so full of menace to free institutions that, rather than submit to it [as Wilson had], a genuine statesman would have died in his tracks" (288). Though American labor had proved its resistance to radicalization, Babbitt saw in leaders like Samuel Gompers a self-serving imperialistic drive. With cowardly politicians like Wilson and exploitive leaders like Gompers, social justice was carrying America toward a "far-off divine event" conceived of as "the domination of the laboring class" (232). There were, however, other serious threats to freedom.

Crusaders and underdogs. Whether the altruists were middle-class Progressives or Christians hoping to save Americans from their own vices, Babbitt enjoined them to mind their own business, to put their "own work before the world's work" (*DL,* 199). He would not distinguish between concern for actual suffering and the self-righteous crusading spirit. Social Gospel preachers with their premillenarian enthusiasm were in his view romantics or utilitarians perverting Christ's message. The danger was that "humanitarian crusaders" were determined "to deprive the individual of every last scrap and vestige of his freedom and finally to subject him to despotic outer control" (296–97). All charities were versions of the Anti-Saloon League, which, by imposing prohibition on the unwilling majority, expressed its "growing will to power and . . . incipient terrorism" (288). Less dangerous but equally foolish were the "socio-religious engineer" and the person who hoped "to save society by turning the crank of a legislative mill" (275) under the delusion that happiness is achievable by manipulating the environment.

In attacking the sentimentalist who bestows "an unselective sympathy on those who have been left behind in the race for economic advantage" (256), Babbitt reminds one of the old Social Darwinists like Herbert Spencer and William Graham Sumner, who considered social reform a pernicious meddling with the law of natural selection, a law supposedly working to perfect the race. The underdog's poverty, Babbitt warned, may be the just punishment for misconduct or laziness. Efforts to uplift the downtrodden may expose the sentimentalist to penalties "visited on those who set out to be kinder than the moral law" (257), penalties which remain unnamed but which are apparently some form of Nemesis brought upon those who preserve society's inferior elements.

Unlike the Social Darwinists, Babbitt neither supported the status quo nor viewed capitalists as the species' fittest. His moral law would not automatically bring some far-off divine event; if followed diligently, however, it might just prevent Armageddon. America must have reform—indeed conversion—in the hearts of those capable of leadership. No lightning-bolt conversion was possible, though; mass inequities and suffering would continue until a natural aristocracy assumed the country's leadership. Only then would social ills find remedy, not by any "sickly sentimentalizing over the lot of the underdog" but by "the moderation and magnanimity of the strong and the successful" (205).

Considering America's enormous social problems, Babbitt's solution seems not only cold-blooded but futile, suited perhaps to Aristotle's polis of a few thousand, but not to an increasingly depersonalized mass society. As Aristotle knew, men of character will rule only in a state small enough so that citizens "know each other's characters; where they do not possess this knowledge, both the election to offices and the decision of lawsuits will go wrong."[23] Nevertheless, Babbitt resisted authoritarianism. Although he shared his fears of the urban masses with many Progressives, he would not accept their eugenic schemes of compulsory birth control and sterilization (intended to save the country from "racial sin"),[24] for he knew eugenics would lead "to a tyranny at once grotesque and ineffectual" (210), just like all schemes for external control. He viewed religious dogmatism, like fascism, as an evil to be considered only as a final, desperate alternative to democracy's *libido dominandi:* "Ultramontane Catholicism does not, like Bolshevism, strike at the very root of civilization. In fact, under certain conditions that are already partly in sight, the Catholic Church may perhaps be the only institution left in the Occident that can . . . uphold civilized standards" (186). Yet even in the face of such knowledge, Babbitt never gave up hope for a humane society in which religion did not mean the death of individualism.

Chapter Six
Humanism and Religion

More than any other issue, humanism's relation to Christianity divided the humanists. T. S. Eliot and More both parted with Babbitt over his rejection of Christian dogma, and even the loyal held widely differing views on the issue. G. R. Elliott urged Babbitt to acknowledge the creed's religious element so humanism could play a part in "an enlightened Catholicity" once Protestantism crumbled. In contrast, Foerster asserted a virtual autonomy. Because humanism preceded Christianity and contained everything essential in it, Foerster argued, humanism "may properly be regarded as *including* religion."[1]

Babbitt's own statements were ambiguous. At times he insisted on a purely positive and critical attitude; at others he asserted that "humanism cannot get along without religion" and that the two are "only different stages in the same path" (*R,* 380). Occasionally, he even called the higher will "ultimately divine" (*DL,* 6). Of course, he often used the term *grace* to describe the mysterious fact that only a few individualists can create standards without recourse to dogma or revelation, but he usually meant only an analogy, asserting a thorough agnosticism and resisting More's efforts to project personality into the beyond.

This issue raises two questions: Was humanism itself a religion in any sense? Could humanism and Christianity ally to unify society and meet its spiritual and emotional needs? These questions cannot be answered with certainty, but enough evidence exists to give a qualified yes to the first question, and, considering the terms in which Babbitt couched his later arguments, a regrettable no to the second.

Humanism as a Religion

Deciding whether humanism was a religion is a problem of definition. Within recent memory, the theologian Michael Novak has argued that sports are a religion because they absorb the spectator

in a significant ritual contest between good and evil. As several
commentators have pointed out, Babbitt's humanism clearly qual-
ifies as a religion if a purely psychological definition is applied.
However, two other reasons suggest humanism was a religion—at
least for Babbitt himself. First, it supplied him with a mythos, or
plot, giving life direction and purpose. Second, it gave him the
sense of a higher being serving in place of the Christian God he
could not know.

Like Foerster, Babbitt thought humanism contained religion's
essential elements, which did not include a superhuman creator.
This may indeed be a crucial exclusion, as Mircea Eliade argues:
"To try to grasp the essence of [religion] by means of physiology,
psychology, sociology, economics, linguistics, art, or any other study,
is false; it misses the one unique and irreducible element in it—
the element of the sacred."[2] Yet Babbitt tried to retain this sacred
element's psychological truth, defining the religious emotions as
awe and humility (as opposed to the Rousseauist's wonder and pride).
At times he reduced religion to a single state: to be "truly religious,"
he wrote, "is only another way of saying [one is] truly humble" (R,
356). Christians humbled themselves before God; Babbitt, before
the great sages and the law of measure.

In a real sense, Babbitt addressed the question of humanism's
relationship to religion in "Buddha and the Occident," written in
1927 for a translation of the Buddhist *Dhammapada*. Here he says
that, unlike easterners, westerners seem "to require faith in a spiritual essence or soul that is sharply set apart from the transitory,
and in a God who is conceived as the supreme 'idea' or entity."[3]
Christianity has, in fact, appropriated Platonism's distinction between a world of unchanging ideas and a transitory world of appearance, a distinction prepared for by the pre-Socratic opposition
between the One and the Many, whose ancient partisans are best
represented by Parmenides and Heraclitus. Buddha, however, refuses to indulge in such metaphysical speculation, denying the im-
mortal Soul and God, for the simple reason that such immutable
entities are not experienceable. Like Babbitt, Buddha is "a critical
and experimental supernaturalist" (D, 236). This means "first of all
that one must deny oneself the luxury of certain affirmations about
ultimate things and start from the immediate data of consciousness"
(D, 236–37). In short, "a personal God and personal immortality"

cannot be affirmed "on strictly experimental grounds" (*D*, 237) and therefore must be denied.

However, what can be affirmed "without going beyond immediate experience and falling into dogma" is the *dhamma*, which Babbitt translates as "human law . . . in contradiction to the law of physical nature" (*D*, 237). Whereas Western philosophy has generally regarded the primary datum either in terms of thinking *(cogito ergo sum)* or feeling *(sentio ergo sum)*, Buddha "gives the primary place to will" (*D*, 237). Both the *cogito* and the *sentio* establish the self or ego as the indubitable standard of Being against which the appearance of all other being is to be measured. For Buddha, however, the thinking and feeling self is but one among other temporary beings in the flux when measured against the higher will. Moreover, in Babbitt's view, the "granting of the primacy to intellect or mind . . . would seem to be incompatible with humility," and to him it seems "a main problem in the spiritual life of the Occident" (*D*, 238).

His denial that the reflective ego is the indubitable ground and measure of Being invites comparison to the nihilistic tradition in Western philosophy, because the nihilistic philosophers, such as Nietzsche, also give the primary place to will. In *The Will to Power* Nietzsche asserts: "We have no categories at all that permit us to distinguish a 'world in itself' from a 'world of appearance.' All our categories of reason are of sensual origin: derived from the empirical world. 'The soul,' 'the ego'—the history of these concepts shows that here, too, the oldest distinction ('breath,' 'life')—."[4] According to Martin Heidegger, for Nietzsche "will as will to power designates the essence of Being" as opposed to Becoming.[5] Buddha, Babbitt, and Nietzsche believe the will alone can impose form upon the flux.

But whereas Buddha finds his guide for the will in the human law, Nietzsche's only guide is desire, which for Babbitt is merely natural impulse. In *Democracy and Leadership* Babbitt interprets Nietzsche's will to power as the "natural will that is . . . released from control" (*DL*, 228), a form of the *libido dominandi* (*DL*, 259). Nietzsche and Buddha seem, in other words, to represent opposing responses to the same "fact" of life. For Nietzsche, "the sensuous world—which in Platonism means the world of semblance and errancy, the realm of error—is the true world"[6] and therefore, through art, must be strenuously asserted. Buddha, however, eschews the false opposition between the world of nature (Becoming, the Many) and a speculative world of Truth (Being, the One) and adheres to the experienceable opposition between the natural law (positive impulse) and the human law (negation and restraint). This opposition is felt as a difference between being driven by desire and being free from desire, and it can be described almost scientifically in terms of moral causes and effects. If one practices restraint, then one achieves happiness. If one follows impulse, then one will be miserable. For Buddha, therefore, the natural self must be subordinated not to a supernatural entity, but to a supernatural law, a human law. Such subordination results in the humility required to achieve the true religious spirit, and to the extent that humanism shares with Buddhism humility, it approaches religion.

As important as humility to the religious nature of humanism are its "fruits." Babbitt once called himself "a sort of pragmatist of the higher will" because he valued experience over authority.[7] However, he recognized two sorts of fruits for two levels of humanism. When defining humanism in its social context, he concerned himself "less with the meditation in which true religion always culminates, than in the mediation or observance of the law of measure that should govern man in his secular relations" (*DL*, 6).

Babbitt never adequately explains the difference between mediation and meditation, but the path from mediation through meditation, ultimately to the nirvana achievable only by the extraordinarily rare Buddha, seems to occur in a series of stages or transitions. The work (*appamada*) of finding the right middle path remains the same, but the issues with which the individual is concerned seem to proceed from the most transitory to the most permanent. In Babbitt, this process seems to depend upon a strenuous refusal to take sides in the various wars of opposites that one encounters. Eventually these conflicts simply no longer arrest the attention, and a new set of conflicts takes their place. Thus "for the Buddhist, emotion, like morality, lies on the way to religion; but as one approaches the goal one enters . . . into a different element . . . " (*D*, 253). Babbitt seems to reserve the term *mediation* for ethical or social issues whose resolution results in a form of outward action; *meditation* he reserves for issues whose resolution results in inaction.

Mediation, possible for many persons, leads to the essential secular virtue—justice. Mediation always involves inner conflict, the "civil war in the cave" observable as "a primordial fact of consciousness"

(*DL,* 10). Meditation raises humanism to a higher plane not easily distinguished from the religious. Babbitt faulted Aristotle for not sufficiently explaining "the bond between the meditative or religious life . . . and the humanistic life or life of mediation" (*R,* 381). It is possible, he believed, "to be a humble and meditative humanist," to be a "man of the world" without being "a mere worldling" (*R,* 380). Aristotle and Buddha exemplified this humanistic-religious life, the one at times achieving the "life of vision," the other at times descending to the level of social duty. The humble and meditative humanist quells the heart's desires and attains peace, not merely justice. Resolving the war in the cave, such a humanist progresses toward "what is more permanent and therefore more peaceful" (*R,* 348) at the center of life. As More recalls, Babbitt in his last days discovered in himself a "fountain of perennial peace and strength,"[8] something approaching the nirvana Buddha achieved in life.

The Humanist Mythos

Having grown up exposed to his father's crank Spiritualism, Babbitt was understandably drawn to Buddhism, "the least mythological of religions" (*DL,* 161). Yet his humanism was not quite so free of mythology nor so divorced from a transcendent being as the more rigorous forms of Buddhism.

David Hoeveler correctly sees the humanists contending with the romantics over the Christian legacy.[9] Babbitt ridiculed romantic "genius" as a "caricature" of Christian grace (*R,* 66) while seeking an equivalent of grace himself, and he condemned the romantic's infinite of outward expansion while asserting the existence of an "inner or human infinite of concentration" (*R,* 251) identified with Dante's image of God at the end of *The Divine Comedy.* Both Babbitt and the romantics thus constructed what M. H. Abrams calls "a displaced and reconstituted theology" and a new, naturalized mythology appropriating Christian patterns. Romantic philosophers and poets were especially drawn to Christianity's union of two pagan myths—the fall from a Golden Age and the eternal recurrence of cycles—into a single finite cycle of fall and rise. The romantic plot—the pattern of history and of the inner life—comprised a fall from unity into division, a circular or upwardly spiraling journey away from and back to home, and the attainment of unity on a higher level. The romantics were not Arcadian dreamers; their higher unity "had been earned by unceasing effort and . . . preserves all the products and powers of intellection and culture."[10]

A similar myth informs Babbitt's own displaced theology. For Babbitt, the fall was an archetypal event reenacted each time a person commits the equivalent of "original sin" by becoming "morally indolent" (R, 153). Babbitt never adequately explains his version of original sin, but an explanation that conforms to his other views would be something like this: When confronting a moral decision, the individual's tendency is to avoid conflict by either blindly rebelling from or by blindly submitting to authority. In either case the terms of choice are not challenged and the difficult labor of mediation is avoided.

A literary illustration of this scene may be found in *Huckleberry Finn* when Huck decides to assist Jim, exclaiming "All right, then, I'll *go* to hell." Huck's is not a true decision but a submission to the stronger of two impulses. Huck has been torn between his sympathy for Jim's plight and his loyalty to his culture's values, and he always follows the line of least resistance. Later Huck's sympathy for Jim quickly fades once he is in the presence of Tom, just as his concern for his culture's values disappears while he is on the raft. Huck's "sin" of moral indolence is most evident when he consciously accepts this false dichotomy. His "decision" is merely an inversion of, and therefore the same as, Rousseau's false dichotomy between the evil of cultural institutions and the goodness of natural man. Huck's "rebellion" against the institutions that supported slavery at the same time confirms the authority of those institutions to damn him. Instead of working centripetally toward a more lawful law that would include Jim, he runs centrifugally way from the law that would exclude him. Huck fails, in short, to create a newer, more central center and only confirms a less central one.

To a humanist such as Babbitt, Huck's failure to engage in the ethical working necessary to establish a new dichotomy, a new standard of conduct, must be considered a product of laziness, moral indolence, rather than an incapacity. The consequences of such indolence are disastrous. Huck remains, as do all the morally indolent, torn between desires whose conflict exists solely as a product of his own laziness. Huck sees but one solution, the romantic's escape, in his case into the American wilderness.

Fallen human beings are necessarily fragmented and must struggle for unity. Although mankind as a whole cannot escape the cycles or pendulum swings of history, in the inner realm the possibility exists for progress, redemption, and transcendence for those who exert the higher will. To "be human" requires the "imposition of form and proportion upon one's expansive impulses" (*R*, 64) by creatively imitating normal human nature. Imposing form becomes "the necessary condition" for possessing the ethical self held "in common with other men" (330). The person who imposes form "grows more at one with himself" and "at the same time tends to enter into communion . . . with those who are submitting to a similar ethical discipline, and . . . moving towards the 'universal centre' " (*DL*, 222).

Because the common self encompasses all who have undergone the same discipline, the great books all seem, in Emerson's phrase, "to be the work of one all-seeing, all-hearing gentleman" (*LC*, 244). There is no sudden apocalypse, but through time the disciplined, creative working of many individuals enters into this omniscient gentleman, and the closest thing to a god Babbitt could ever worship assumes human form. The experience is profoundly religious; it ministers to a "deep need of human nature—the need to lose itself in a larger whole" (*R*, 166).

To impose form is simultaneously to journey down a "path," to "increase in peace, poise, centrality" (*R*, 252), and to create an eternal self that is also a civilized kingdom. For Babbitt, "civilization" must be "deliberately willed . . . first of all by the individual in his own heart" (*DL*, 229). Civilization depends on "the forms of inner action" (*DL*, 229)—another way of saying that "the kingdom of heaven is within" (*R*, 289). If humanism has an eschatology, then "civilization" is the end toward which the whole creation moves, or rather would move if men and women willed it. When they fail to achieve the civilized condition ("urbanity"), they risk "being numbered with the immense multitude that Dante saw in the vestibule of Hell" (*DL*, 25).

Ironically, in general outline this myth resembles the late prophetic works of William Blake, whom Babbitt considered quite mad. Blake's Eden was an eternal city, not a happy garden, and the apocalypse brought "Jerusalem," the civilized kingdom that constituted Jesus's larger human body. Blake set man over nature and vilified Bacon and Rousseau. According to his cyclical vision of

history, indolent imagination causes civilizations to fall into naturalism and brutal warfare. In *Jerusalem* Blake's eternal man Albion
falls into division when his imagination fails and he denies his unity
in Jesus by proclaiming *"We are not One: we are Many."* Thereafter,
Los (conscious creative effort) and Satan (natural life) struggle for
possession of Luvuh (redeemable man). With the triumph of Los,
Luvuh and the other fragments of man—Urizen, Tharmas, and
Urthona—unite in the bosom of Albion, who walks "To & fro in
Eternity as One Man." The poem's final vision is the timeless city
externalizing the restored inner unity of the One Man and constituted by all of mankind's creative acts—"All Human Forms identified"—which "are named Jerusalem."[11]

Babbitt and Blake differed greatly in their emphases, and Babbitt's myth is dispersed rather than cohering in a single progressive
narrative. Nevertheless, it constitutes a discernible pattern (there
may be others) amid the masses of allusions and quotations that
make up his books. As Frye asserts at the end of *Anatomy of Criticism,*
the further one takes the language of discourse in an effort to explain
a reality above ordinary experience, the more clearly mythic patterns
show through.[12] Drawing on the same Christian tradition, Babbitt's
philosophical works and Blake's prophetic poems, despite their generic differences, converge on their inner form, on an imaginatively
grasped vision of human nature.

The question remains how literally Babbitt took this mythical
eternal self. More accused him, in fact, of flirting with "modernism
of the *als-ob* [as-if] type" by refusing to speculate about the reality
of spirit. The reference was to theories such as Hans Vaihinger's
Philosophy of As-If, which considers natural laws, abstract ideas, and
ethical norms merely "fictions" creating an illusory order and purpose. Babbitt, however, thought fictions ungrounded in reality were
pernicious. For example, the French syndicalist George Sorel's mythical general strike stirred unrest among Europe's working class and
threatened class war. To Babbitt, Sorel's fiction was a "Jesuitical"
falsehood; religions and myths should embody "vital truth instead
of vital error" and produce reverence and restraint.[13] He believed
his "One" to be a vital truth, and when More wrote him questioning
the Buddhist doctrine of the nonexistence of the soul, he explained
in print that Buddha had really just adopted a "practical" (*D,* 240)
strategy to keep his followers from a sense of false security. Buddha's

nirvana was not annihilation or nonexistence, he claimed, but "the eternal," a goal Babbitt sought himself (*D, 239*).

In Babbitt's mind, then, the eternal "divine" self was somehow real, transcending the individual, though it could be known only imperfectly in rare visionary moments. Babbitt thus seems to have embraced a species of idealism. Although he rejected Platonic ideas, Rousseau's higher unity of emotions, or Hegel's higher unity of intellect, he accepted a higher unity of will, suggesting an influence from his closest friend at Harvard, the idealist philosopher Josiah Royce.[14]

Babbitt found a friendly adversary in Royce, who ardently supported the modern university and preached humanitarian public service. Babbitt, however, always grounded his friendships in shared beliefs. Despite their differences, the two men were both westerners and Harvard outsiders who shared a strong sense of duty and professed a philosophy of the absolute to counter modern relativism.

In his best-known work, *The Philosophy of Loyalty* (published the same year as *Literature and the American College*), Royce argues that human beings longing for commitment and community often pass through something very like Babbitt's naturalistic, humanistic, and religious levels. In Royce's scheme the natural self is a chaotic play of impulses, but through imitation one learns to organize these impulses and become a social being. However, one becomes a true person only by freely choosing a cause giving life centrality and purpose. Loyalty is never slavery to convention; like Babbitt's sound individualists, the loyal simply temper freedom with a sense of duty. Loyalty requires constant effort, yet leads to peace and fulfillment. The devotion to cause becomes "a mysterious higher or deeper self" serving as a moral standard, a conscience, an equivalent of grace. The united wills of those in the same cause become "a sort of supernatural being," a form of the Absolute.[15]

The Absolute Will is aristocratic. Although it wants to organize all persons in a "Great Community," this community, like Babbitt's civilization, cannot be realized; never rising above their natural selves, many are doomed to the unregenerate's weeping and gnashing of teeth. Only a few achieve salvation in the Great Community by conquering original sin, the deficiency "in attention to the demands of the ethical will."[16]

Royce's loyalty to the Great Community surely describes Babbitt's own commitment to the community of humanists past and present. However, neither he nor Royce claimed to know the fate of the individual consciousness; it was enough for Babbitt that purposeful work led to inner peace. As More recognized, few persons could accept such a faith. To paraphrase Whitman in "Song of Myself," it made death seem different than anyone had supposed, but certainly not luckier than most had hoped.

Humanism, Church and State

According to More, Babbitt's concern for tactics kept him from expressing his true antipathy toward the institutional church, which he valued largely for its influence on conduct. He may also have learned a lesson from Charles Maurras and the reactionary *Action Française*. During an 1897 summer in Paris Babbitt had attended lectures by this group and, when writing *Literature and the American College,* he had drawn encouragement from Pierre Lasserre and other traditionalist critics of romanticism. Eventually, however, he recognized the *Action Française* as a proto-fascist party whose gang of thugs contributed to France's social instability. Maurras's worst tactical blunder was defending the Catholic church as a national tradition while openly ridiculing its supernaturalism. This cynical effort to use the church as a political instrument brought a papal condemnation in 1927, a crushing blow just when the party was gaining popular support. [17] Babbitt avoided a similar blunder. Except, perhaps, for the abortive attempts of 1930, he resisted formal organization, and he never argued that humanism was superior to religion, though he was probably closer to Foerster than to Elliott on this question.

Wanting a unified society, Babbitt knew the impossibility of returning to the Middle Ages, when the symbols of heaven and hell ruled the imagination and united everyone "from the top to the bottom of society in the same spiritual hopes and fears" (*DL,* 28). To be sure, the old symbols still governed the imaginations of Catholics and fundamentalist Protestants, but Babbitt viewed the ancient dogmas as the most desperate means of staving off barbarism (he considered the fundamentalists' vengeful Christ of the second coming a vicarious expression of repressed *libido dominandi* that made "Nero and Caligula seem respectable" [*DL,* 141]). New symbols were therefore necessary if society were to have both vital control and individualism.

Valuing the man of character's symbolic power, Babbitt in his last years cherished hopes that liberal Protestantism could help produce such men. Influenced by romantic and Darwinian currents of thought, liberal Protestant theologians in the late nineteenth century demythologized Christianity, downplaying the atonement, treating Christ primarily as an ethical teacher, and looking to the kingdom of God in this world. In H. Richard Niebuhr's words, they envisioned "A God without wrath [who] brought men without sin into a kingdom without judgment through the ministrations of a Christ without a Cross."[18] Babbitt hated these developments because without a sense of sin Christians were losing their humility and becoming humanitarian crusaders. Nevertheless, liberal Protestants often possessed a nondogmatic, ecumenical spirit to which the humanists might appeal.

In "Buddha and the Occident" Babbitt treats Buddha as a psychologist superior to modern psychoanalysts and behaviorists. To an extent, he argues, Buddhism and Christianity both aim at psychological adjustment, though Buddhism offers a better way of attaining it. "Everything," he writes, "will be found to hinge finally on the idea of meditation" (*D*, 270). Christians who meditated would achieve something of Buddha's insight and Christ's humility. Indirectly, then, Babbitt was challenging so-called Christians to rise to his own spiritual level, to experience their own faith's truth and thus become exemplary men of character.

Unfortunately, humanism offered little imaginative appeal to those who could neither create their own standards nor believe in heaven and hell. His creed appealed most to those seeking spiritual conversion—men like More, Foerster, Elliott, and Sherman. Still, he believed leaping from the naturalistic to the religious level could enslave one to a sham religion. Thus he offered a humanism demanding only "moderate and sensible and decent" (*R*, xxi) conduct, something "more within our capacity than religion" (*DL*, 195). Emulating ethical leaders and adhering to social conventions would produce happiness, though to avoid formalism the conventions must be held "flexibly, imaginatively, and, as it were, progressively" (*DL*, 301).

Such a life would be like walking a tightrope in a high wind, so Babbitt provides a moral balance pole—habit. Exercising the higher will means pulling back on impulse until a habit is formed and "at last the new direction given to the natural man becomes automatic and unconscious. The humanistic worker may thus acquire at last the spontaneity in right doing that the beautiful soul professes to have received as a free gift from 'nature' " (R, 386). This argument echoes the *Nicomachean Ethics,* where Aristotle asserts that "moral virtue comes about as a result of habit" and that right education produces pleasure in the exercise of habitual virtue.[19] However, Babbitt sails dangerously close to the shoals of naturalism, for his humanist worker seems like a Baconian behaviorist's well-adjusted automaton reaping the spontaneous Rousseauist's emotional satisfactions.

To an extent, such objections are unfair. After all, continuous mediation would soon create unbearable anxiety. Habits get people through the day; mediation and higher will are needed only to deal with new moral problems. Habits become part of character, reduce anxiety, and keep one close to the human norm. Like the Puritans, who believed that right habit prepares one for grace, Babbitt saw in habit, especially habitual meditation, a means of attaining spiritual insight. Yet, like the Puritans, he was as much concerned with controlling the unregenerate. He would "oppose no obstacles to those who are rising above the conventional level, but would resist firmly those who are sinking beneath it" (R, 388). Only a sound education—and by this he meant more than formal schooling—could keep people from sinking.

There are disturbing implications to Babbitt's later statements on education. *Literature and the American College* had exalted the imaginative and intellectual life achieved by assimilation and reflection. *Rousseau and Romanticism* and *Democracy and Leadership,* both reflecting the turmoil of the Great War and its aftermath, defend the right of children to be "born into a cosmos" and not "pitchforked into chaos" (R, 388) as Dewey would have them be. To protect civilization, which may "consist above all in an orderly transmission of right habits" (R, 387), men and women must establish a convention regarding the habits they would transmit.

Babbitt was countering the extremes of his age with an opposite extreme, while recognizing the difficulty of attaining equilibrium: "The combining of convention with a due respect for the liberty of the individual involves, it must be admitted, adjustments of the utmost delicacy" (DL, 300). Insisting on right habits does not seem a delicate adjustment, and it suggests his ultimate despair for an enduring humanist society. Education that prevents the child from becoming "the prisoner of bad habits" (R, 387) may create a prisoner of good habits and is not likely to produce many sound individualists. Perhaps Babbitt believed the saving remnant would always rise above its environment, but the danger of formalism is great. At that point the humanist must himself undergo conversion, pull in the direction of freedom and imaginative play, or the violent release of "repressed and thwarted" (*DL,* 140) energies that produced the French Revolution will bring Armageddon.

Nevin calls humanism a "halfway house" religion because Babbitt wanted "to dispense with the old terrors of orthodoxy and yet keep the sublimity of the religious sense" while his aristocratic higher will left most people to their hellish lower selves.[20] However, Nevin overlooks Babbitt's belief that convention and dogmatic religion constitute forms of the higher will. In Babbitt's humanistic society a few persons with a sublime religious sense would constitute the leadership class. At the bottom would be a large substrate ruled by the hopes and terrors of orthodoxy. And in between would be a yet larger mass of spiritually inert, but "happy" automatons living by their socially approved habits, imitating superior men, and measuring out their lives in coffee spoons.

In 1933 and then again in 1973 intellectuals calling themselves humanists issued manifestos professing faith in reason, technology, and brotherly love. The more recent secular humanists, wanting "the whole person fulfilled," called for "scientific intelligence" balanced by "the cultivation of feeling and love."[21] But where, Babbitt would ask, is the cultivation of character and wisdom? This new humanism is merely the old scientific and sentimental humanitarianism in modern dress. But even so, it might be objected, the dream of a world united in love surely offers more food for the soul than the moral realist's acceptance of human incapacity. But for Babbitt, equality meant a deadly mediocrity leaving no place for the extraordinary, for the experience of awe. He saw in his humanist equivalent of grace the same beauty his Puritan ancestors saw in their own terrible doctrine of election. As Perry Miller writes in explaining the Puritan's stern faith, it left "room in the universe for a free and unpredictable power, for a lawless force that flashes through the night in unexpected brilliance and unaccountable majesty. It was better . . . that most men be passed over by this illumination . . . than that all men should be born without the hope of beholding it, or that a few should forgo the ecstasy of the vision."[22]

Notes and References

Chapter One

1. Paul Elmer More quoted from Frederick Manchester and Odell Shepard, ed., *Irving Babbitt: Man and Teacher* (1941; reprint, New York: Greenwood Press, 1969), 325. This book collects thirty-nine memorial essays that constitute the richest source of information about Babbitt. Henceforth it will be cited as *Man and Teacher*, preceded by the name of the contributor. Babbitt is treated as a born conservative by J. David Hoeveler, "Babbitt and Contemporary Conservative Thought in America," *Modern Age* 28 (Spring/Summer 1984):189. The other quotations are from H. L. Mencken, *Prejudices: Second Series* (New York: Alfred A. Knopf, 1920), 19, 23; Austin Warren, *New England Saints* (Ann Arbor: University of Michigan Press, 1956), v.

2. George A. Panichas, "Babbitt and Religion," *Modern Age* 28 (Spring/Summer 1984):178.

3. Ann Douglas, *The Feminization of American Culture* (New York: Alfred A. Knopf, 1977), 5, 9.

4. *Literature and the American College: Essays in Defense of the Humanities* (Boston and New York: Houghton, Mifflin & Co., 1908), 173; hereafter cited parenthetically in the text as *LC* followed by page number. For a discussion of the concern for strenuousness in this period, see Grant C. Knight, *The Strenuous Age in American Literature* (Chapel Hill: University of North Carolina Press, 1954).

5. Sadie Mahon Malsbary, undated letter to Dora Drew Babbitt. The letter was probably written about 1934, when Mrs. Babbitt was collecting materials for a possible biography of her husband. The account of Babbitt's early life given in this chapter is based largely on these materials, which until recently were in the possession of the Babbitt family and now reside in the Babbitt Papers at the Harvard University Archives. So that readers will not be distracted by an excessive number of notes, only significant direct quotations from these materials will be documented. Edwin Babbitt is quoted from a letter to Irving Babbitt, 24 September 1885, in the Babbitt Papers.

6. For a discussion of the boys' gang, see Alfred Habegger, *Gender, Fantasy, and Realism in American Literature* (New York: Columbia University Press, 1982), 206–19. According to Habegger, the gang "virtually formed a complete society, with seasonal rituals and a tough, arbitrary, inflexible, and barbaric system of rules. No boy who cared to be respected

143

by other boys (and nobody else counted) could afford to slight these rules"
(214).

7. Sadie Mahon Malsbary, undated letter to Dora Drew Babbitt.
For Babbitt's youthful adventures, see Mrs. Babbitt's biographical sketch
in *Man and Teacher,* ix-xi.

8. Tom Babbitt to Irving Babbitt, 24 August 1884, Babbitt Papers.

9. "The American Cow-boy," Theme III, 16 November 1886, Babbitt Papers.

10. Edwin D. Babbitt to Irving Babbitt, 25 June 1885, Babbitt
Papers.

11. Edwin D. Babbitt, *Religion as Revealed by the Material and Spiritual
Universe* (New York: Babbitt & Co., 1881), 230, 59, 55, 86.

12. R. Laurence Moore, *In Search of White Crows: Spiritualism, Para-
psychology, and American Culture* (New York: Oxford University Press,
1977), 120; Edwin D. Babbitt, *Religion,* 71.

13. Moore, *Spiritualism,* 7, 19–24.

14. Edwin D. Babbitt, *The Principles of Light and Color,* ed. Faber
Birren (Secaucus, N.J.: Citadel Press, 1980), 261; Babbitt, *Religion,* 236–
37.

15. Babbitt, *Religion,* 68, 87–88.

16. Burton Rascoe, "Pupils of Polonius," in *The Critique of Humanism:
A Symposium,* ed. C. Hartley Grattan (New York: Brewer & Warren, 1930),
127; Irving Babbitt, *Rousseau and Romanticism* (Boston and New York:
Houghton Mifflin Co., 1919), 157, 159. Henceforth cited parenthetically
in the text as *R* followed by page number.

17. Babbitt, *Religion,* 101, 124. In a telephone conversation on 3
April 1986, Edward S. Babbitt told one of the authors that his father also
accepted Edwin's faith in the virtues of sunlight and took sunbaths in
hopes of reversing the course of his last illness.

18. William F. Giese in *Man and Teacher,* 8–9; Edwin Babbitt to
Irving Babbitt, 18 March 1886, Babbitt Papers. The practical joke is
recounted in Irving's freshman essay "Eastern vs. Western Journalism."
With tongue in cheek, he denies descending to personalities as a reporter
though "To be sure, I once had an item inserted in the paper about a
certain friend to the effect that he had committed suicide by cutting his
throat with a razor and bleeding over a tub."

19. Babbitt's dormitory is described in an undated typescript by
Giese in the Babbitt Papers. Giese describes their first meeting and their
summer of reading, discussion, and hiking through New Hampshire in
1886. Babbitt's views on the classics are found in a freshman essay on
"The Emotional Element in the Classics." Strangely, at this time he found
the difference between modern and classical writers to be "the predomi-

nance of the emotional over the intellectual and moral" in the classics. He would later reverse this judgment.

20. Giese in *Man and Teacher*, 1–4.

21. The quotation is from a brief intellectual autobiography Babbitt wrote in 1929 for possible inclusion in Norman Foerster's collection of essays *Humanism and American* (1930). The eleven-page holograph, now in the Babbitt Papers, will henceforth be cited as "Autobiography."

22. "My 'Aim' in Life," Theme I, 12 October 1886, Babbitt Papers.

23. "The Light of Asia," Theme VII, 25 January 1887, Babbitt Papers. The essay deals with Edwin Arnold's epic on the life of Buddha. Babbitt hints at some personal mystical experiences when he introduces a quotation dealing with "being's ceaseless tide": "The opening lines are full of meaning to those who are familiar with certain phases in modern thought and have had certain mental experiences themselves." Giese quoted from *Man and Teacher*, 10.

24. Giese, undated typescript, Babbitt Papers; Aristotle, *Nicomachean Ethics* 1098b and 1104a. As we have seen, in high school Babbitt was already arguing for the mean, but according to "Autobiography," it was at Harvard that he got "a pretty thorough saturation" in the classics.

25. Matthew Arnold, *Culture and Anarchy,* ed. R. H. Super (Ann Arbor: University of Michigan Press, 1965), 102.

26. Edwin D. Babbitt to Irving Babbitt, 24 May 1889, Babbitt Papers.

27. From Babbitt's application for graduate study in his student records in the Harvard Archives.

28. Charles William Eliot, *Educational Reform: Essays and Addresses* (1898; reprint, New York: Arno Press and New York Times, 1969), 227; G. Stanley Hall, "Research the Vital Spirit of Teaching," *Forum* 17 (1894):565.

29. Rollo Walter Brown, *Harvard Yard in the Golden Age* (New York: Current Books, 1948), 100, 93.

30. Babbitt's notebooks are in the Babbitt Papers. Norton's son is quoted in Warren, *New England Saints,* 130.

31. Telegram, Babbitt Papers.

32. Irving Babbitt to the Faculty of Arts and Sciences, Harvard University, 17 March 1892. This letter is part of his application for a graduate fellowship in his student records in the Harvard Archives.

33. Irving Babbitt to Charles R. Lanman, 8 April 1892, in Babbitt's student records, Harvard Archives.

34. Joseph M. Kitagawa, "The History of Religions *(Religionswissenschaft)* Then and Now," *The History of Religions,* ed. Joseph M. Kitagawa (New York: Macmillan Publishing Co., 1985), 133–34, 136.

35. "Autobiography."

36. *Spanish Character and Other Essays,* ed. Frederick Manchester, Rachel Giese, and William F. Giese (Boston and New York: Houghton Mifflin & Co., 1940), 153. The discussion of Buddhism is based on Walpola Rahula, *What the Buddha Taught,* 2d ed. rev. (New York: Grove Press, 1974). Rahula's humanistic bent and reliance on the early Pali canon parallel Babbitt's own practice.

37. Quoted in Arthur Hazard Dakin, *Paul Elmer More* (Princeton: Princeton University Press, 1960), 41.

38. Paul Elmer More in *Man and Teacher,* 323.

39. Quoted in Dakin, *More,* 314, 45.

40. Aristotle, *Nicomachean Ethics* 1113a; Norton quoted in Warren, *Saints,* 124; More quoted in Dakin, *More,* 48.

41. Frank Jewett Mather, Jr., in *Man and Teacher,* 45; Babbitt, to Paul Elmer More, 8 December 1913. This letter is from a typescript of the Babbitt-More correspondence prepared and edited by Dora Drew Babbitt in the 1930s. It resides in the Babbitt Papers and henceforth will be cited as the Babbitt-More Correspondence.

42. Minutes of the French Department, 19 May 1894, Harvard Archives. The next meeting of the Department was 7 December 1894, indicating that Babbitt's appointment was made without the usual vote of the members.

43. Babbitt to More, 23 December 1895, Babbitt-More Correspondence.

44. Minutes of the French Department, 3 February 1897, Harvard Archives.

45. Babbitt to More, 23 December 1895, and 5 March 1896, Babbitt-More Correspondence; Giese in *Man and Teacher,* 4; Babbitt to More, 6 May 1897, Babbitt-More Correspondence.

46. Minutes of the French Department, 28 March 1899, Harvard Archives. The proposal was presented to the Department in the meeting of 18 March 1898.

47. William F. Maag, Jr. in *Man and Teacher,* 61–62; Stuart Pratt Sherman in *Man and Teacher,* 89–90.

48. Babbitt to More, 5 March 1896, Babbitt-More Correspondence.

49. Babbitt to More, 17 May 1908, Babbitt-More Correspondence.

50. Babbitt to More, 9 October 1910, Babbitt-More Correspondence.

51. A. Lawrence Lowell to Babbitt, 13 March 1911, Babbitt Papers.

52. J. D. M. Ford to Babbitt, 14 March 1911, Babbitt Papers; More in *Man and Teacher,* 330.

53. A. Lawrence Lowell to More, 20 March 1911, Babbitt Papers. More's comment is handwritten in the margins of this letter, which he

evidently forwarded to Babbitt. The late request from Illinois is in a letter
from D. H. Carnahan dated 30 January 1913, Babbitt Papers.

54. Babbitt to More, 2 June 1896, Babbitt-More Correspondence;
the facts about Babbitt's marriage were supplied by Edward S. Babbitt in
an interview on 15 June 1985. Unless otherwise indicated, the biographical
facts in the following paragraphs are drawn from this interview. The in-
ferences are the authors'.

55. Royce's and Babbitt's health problems are discussed in letters
from Babbitt to More, 13 February 1912, and 12 February 1915, Babbitt-
More Correspondence.

56. From Babbitt's Notes on Miscellaneous Readings, Babbitt Papers.

57. More to Dora Drew Babbitt, 10 March 1934, Babbitt Papers.

58. Giese to Esther Babbitt, 27 June 1933, Babbitt Papers, and in
Man and Teacher, 25.

59. Edmund Wilson, "Notes on Babbitt and More," in *The Critique
of Humanism*, 49.

60. "Self-Reliance," in *The Collected Works of Ralph Waldo Emerson*,
ed. Joseph Slater, Alfred R. Ferguson, and Jean Ferguson Carr (Cambridge
and London: Harvard University Press, 1979), 2:42.

Chapter Two

1. *The Masters of Modern French Criticism* (Boston and New York:
Houghton Mifflin Co., 1912), 362. Hereafter cited parenthetically in the
text as *M*.

2. What follows is summarized from Stephen R. Yarbrough, "Jonathan Edwards on Rhetorical Authority," *Journal of the History of Ideas* 47
(July–September 1986):395–408.

3. Thomas R. Nevin, *Irving Babbitt: An Intellectual Study* (Chapel
Hill and London: University of North Carolina Press, 1984), 8.

4. William James, *The Will to Believe and Other Essays on Popular
Philosophy* (New York: Dover Publications, 1956), 11.

5. Ibid., 212.

6. William James, *The Varieties of Religious Experience* (New York:
Mentor Books, 1961), 375.

7. Alburey Castell, editor's introduction to William James, *Essays
in Pragmatism* (New York: Hafner Publishing Co., 1948), x.

8. Patrick Kiaran Dooley, *Pragmaticism as Humanism: The Philosophy
of William James* (Chicago: Nelson Hall, 1974).

9. *The Letters of William James*, ed. Henry James, 2 vols. (Boston:
Atlantic Monthly Press, 1970), 1:147. Quoted in Dooley, *Pragmaticism*, 63.

10. Dooley, *Pragmaticism*, 64.

11. William James, *The Principles of Psychology,* 2 vols. (New York: Dover, 1950), 2:567.

12. James, *Will to Believe,* 205.

13. James, *Principles,* 2:672.

14. *On Being Creative and Other Essays* (New York: Biblo & Tannen, 1968), xiv; hereafter cited parenthetically in the text as *O* followed by page number.

15. *The New Laokoon: An Essay on the Confusion of the Arts* (Boston and New York: Houghton Mifflin Co., 1910), 202; hereafter cited parenthetically in the text as *NL* followed by page number.

16. Nevin, *Babbitt,* 152, n. 9.

17. Claes E. Ryn, "Babbitt and the Problem of Reality," *Modern Age* 28 (Spring/Summer, 1984):161.

18. Ibid., 162.

19. Ibid., 161.

20. Ibid., 162.

21. T. S. Eliot, *Selected Essays,* 2d ed. (New York: Harcourt, Brace & World, 1950), 425.

22. Ibid., 421.

23. Ibid., 428.

24. *Ryn,* "Babbitt and . . . Reality," 158.

25. *Spanish Character and Other Essays,* 235; hereafter cited parenthetically in the text as *SC* followed by page number.

26. Allen Tate, "The Fallacy of Humanism," in *The Critique of Humanism,* 141.

27. Henry Hazlitt, "Humanism and Value," in *Critique of Humanism,* 95.

28. See for example Harry Salpeter, "A Portrait of Irving Babbitt," *Commonweal* 24 (1936): 234–36.

29. Babbitt to G. R. Elliott, 15 September 1919.

30. Ryn, "Babbitt and . . . Reality," 157.

31. Ibid.

32. Claes E. Ryn, "The Humanism of Irving Babbitt Revisited," *Modern Age* 21 (Summer 1977):254.

33. For a good discussion of Arthur Lovejoy's criticisms of Babbitt's treatment of Schiller, and Babbitt's response to them, see Nevin, *Babbitt,* 51–52.

34. Babbitt to More, 22 September 1927, Babbitt-More Correspondence. Quoted from Nevin, *Babbitt,* 52.

35. Nevin, *Babbitt,* 43.

36. Ibid.

37. Ibid., 62.

38. Ibid., 60.

39. *Masters,* 240; Nevin, *Babbitt,* 60.

40. Nevin, *Babbitt,* 62.

41. Ibid.

Chapter Three

1. Henry F. May, *The End of American Innocence: A Study of the First Years of Our Own Time, 1912–1917* (1959; reprint, Oxford: Oxford University Press, 1979), 57–58, 298–99.

2. William Maag in *Man and Teacher,* 68.

3. Many accounts of Babbitt's classroom manner appear in *Man and Teacher.* See, for example, those of R. T. Mei, 114–16; Austin Warren, 209–13; Hoffman Nickerson, 91–92. The clipping on the "beautiful soul" is in Babbitt's class notes in the Babbitt Papers.

4. Babbitt to More, 1 and 10 April 1906, Babbitt-More Correspondence; *Masters,* 344; T. S. Eliot in *Man and Teacher,* 102.

5. From lecture notes in the Babbitt Papers, 1 October 1925.

6. See the following in *Man and Teacher:* Brooks Otis, 307; Gordon K. Chalmers, 289; Alan R. Thompson, 225; Theodore Spencer, 282.

7. Austin Warren in *Man and Teacher,* 209–12.

8. Quoted in J. David Hoeveler, Jr., *The New Humanism: A Critique of Modern America, 1900–1940* (Charlottesville: University Press of Virginia, 1977), 16.

9. Foerster to Babbitt, 29 December 1919, Babbitt Papers.

10. T. S. Eliot, "Tradition and the Individual Talent," in *Literary Opinion in America,* ed. Morton Dauwen Zabel (1937; rev. New York: Harper & Brothers, 1951), 94, 97; Eliot in *Man and Teacher,* 104.

11. G. R. Elliott to Babbitt, 24 May 1918.

12. *Masters,* 352; *NL,* 240.

13. Babbitt to More, 3 July 1907, Babbitt-More Correspondence; Nevin, *Babbitt,* 39.

14. Babbitt to More, 31 December 1908, 14 March 1915, Babbitt-More Correspondence; G. R. Elliott to Babbitt, 16 February 1929.

15. Babbitt to More, 11 June 1908, Babbitt-More Correspondence; More to Babbitt, 31 October 1907, Babbitt-More Correspondence; G. R. Elliott in *Man and Teacher,* 162.

16. Babbitt to More, 5 December 1912, 13 February 1916, Babbitt-More Correspondence.

17. *LC,* 166; *R,* xxiii, xxi.

18. Louis Trenchard More, "The Pretensions of Science," in *Humanism and America: Essays on the Outlook of Modern Civilisation,* ed. Norman Foerster (New York: Farrar & Rinehart, 1930), 16. The quotation from More's *Demon of the Absolute* is from Chapter 5 as reprinted in *Humanism*

and America under the title "The Humility of Common Sense" (see p. 68).

19. Barton and Ford quoted in William E. Leuchtenburg, *The Perils of Prosperity, 1914–1932* (Chicago and London: University of Chicago Press, 1958), 189, 176.

20. Paul Elmer More to Babbitt, 14 September 1917, Babbitt-More Correspondence; Babbitt to More, 21 November 1917, Babbitt-More Correspondence.

21. Babbitt to More, 13 September 1922, ibid.

22. Gordon Keith Chalmers in *Man and Teacher,* 291.

23. Paul Elmer More, ibid., 326.

24. Lawrence Buell, *Literary Transcendentalism: Style and Vision in the American Renaissance* (Ithaca and London: Cornell University Press, 1973), 75–139.

25. W. K. Wimsatt, Jr., *The Prose Style of Samuel Johnson* (1941; reprint, New Haven and London: Yale University Press, 1963), 101, 46, 47.

26. Irving Babbitt, *Democracy and Leadership* (Boston and New York: Houghton Mifflin Company, 1924), p. 97; hereafter cited parenthetically in the text as *DL* followed by page number.

27. From undated and untitled typescript/manuscript in the Babbitt Papers. References in the text place this lecture about 1932.

28. Babbitt to More, 27 April 1919, Babbitt-More Correspondence.

29. Alvin Kernan, *The Cankered Muse: Satire of the English Renaissance* (New Haven: Yale University Press, 1959), 7–8.

30. Ibid., 14, 21.

31. Babbitt to More, 4 September 1919, Babbitt-More Correspondence.

32. Babbitt to More, 23 May 1917; "Genius and Taste," *Nation* 106 (February 1918): 141; J. E. Spingarn to Babbitt, 21 February 1918, Babbitt Papers.

33. Wilfred Parsons, S. J., "What is this New Humanism?" *America,* 12 April 1930, 21. Copy in the Babbitt Papers.

34. H. L. Mencken, "The Library," *American Mercury* 18 (September-December 1929): 123; "The Critic and American Life," in *On Being Creative and Other Essays* (Boston: Houghton Mifflin, 1932), 204; More quoted in Dakin, *Paul Elmer More,* 258; Upton Sinclair to Seward Collins, 16 January 1930 (carbon copy in the Babbitt Papers).

35. Seward Collins, "Criticism in America. III. The End of the Anti-Humanist Myth," *Bookman* 72 (1930–31): 163; Brody quoted in Hoeveler, *New Humanism,* 24.

36. These efforts are revealed in a letter from Royce to Irving Babbitt

dated 14 May 1914. Apparently Babbitt and Royce were dealing with Herbert Weir Smyth, Eliot Professor of Greek, who was proud of his German Ph.D. from Göttingen (see Samuel Morison, ed., *The Development of Harvard University since the Inauguration of President Eliot, 1869–1929* [Cambridge: Harvard University Press, 1930], 37 n). Babbitt's feelings about his election to the French Institute were conveyed to one of the authors by Edward S. Babbitt in a telephone conversation in the spring of 1986.

37. Babbitt to More, 4 January 1920; More to Babbitt, 17 January 1920; Babbitt to More, 10 August 1921 (all in the Babbitt-More Correspondence); More to Maurice Baum, 9 June 1924 (quoted in Dakin, *More,* 221).

38. Babbitt to More, 14 May 1924, Babbitt-More Correspondence; More in *Man and Teacher,* 330.

39. Babbitt to More, 14 May 1924, Babbitt-More Correspondence; Dakin, *More,* 242.

40. Babbitt to More, 21 November 1917; More to Babbitt, 2 January 1922, both in Babbitt-More Correspondence.

41. T. S. Eliot, *For Lancelot Andrewes: Essays On Style and Order* (Garden City, N.Y.: Doubleday, Doran & Co., 1929), vii; Babbitt to More, 25 December 1928, Babbitt-More Correspondence.

42. Eliot, *For Lancelot Andrewes,* 145; Eliot, "Religion Without Humanism," in *Humanism and America,* 107–8. For a discussion of Eliot's role in the debates of the 1920s, see John D. Margolis, *T. S. Eliot's Intellectual Development, 1922–1939* (Chicago and London: University of Chicago Press, 1972), 53–67, 118–28.

43. Babbitt to More, 3 July 1928, Babbitt-More Correspondence.

44. Babbitt to Norman Foerster, 30 July 1924 (transcribed by Dora Drew Babbitt) and 15 October 1928, Babbitt Papers.

45. Babbitt to Foerster, 19 February 1929, Babbitt Papers.

46. Babbitt to Foerster, 24 March 1929, 16 December 1928, Babbitt Papers; Warner Rice in *Man and Teacher,* 263; Babbitt to Foerster, 26 August 1929, Babbitt Papers.

47. Theodore Spencer in *Man and Teacher,* 283.

48. Foerster to Babbitt, 20 September 1929, Babbitt Papers; the publisher's notice quoted from Hoeveler, *New Humanism,* 26 n. 37.

49. Odell Shepard to Babbitt, 7 January 1930, Babbitt Papers.

50. Joseph Wood Krutch, *The Modern Temper: A Study and a Confession* (1929; reprint, New York: Harcourt, Brace & World, Harvest, 1956), 26.

51. John Crowe Ransom, et al., *I'll Take My Stand: The South and the Agrarian Tradition* (1930; reprint, Baton Rouge and London: Louisiana State University Press, 1980), xliv.

52. Alfred Kazin, *On Native Grounds: An Interpretation of Modern American Prose Literature* (New York: Harcourt, Brace & Co., 1942), 291.

Chapter Four

1. For more information on the development of English departments, see William Riley Parker, "Where Do English Departments Come From?" *College English* 28 (February 1967):339–51.

2. Soon after taking office, Charles William Eliot, president of Harvard, initiated the elective system [see "The New Education," *Atlantic Monthly* 23 (February 1869):203–20, 358–67]. Babbitt, who had felt the full force of this policy, wrote a scathing attack on the system after Eliot's death ["President Eliot and American Education," *Forum* 81 (January 1929): 1–10.

3. R. S. Crane, "History Versus Criticism in the University Study of Literature," *English Journal: College Edition* 24 (October 1935):645–67.

4. John Crowe Ransom, *The World's Body* (Charles Scribner's Sons, 1938; reprint, Baton Rouge: Louisiana State University Press, 1968), 327–50.

5. William K. Wimsatt, Jr. and Cleanth Brooks, *Literary Criticism: A Short History,* 2 vols. (Chicago and London: University of Chicago Press, 1957), 2:451.

6. T. S. Eliot, "Experiment in Criticism," *Bookman* 60 (November 1929):230.

7. Wimsatt and Brooks, *Literary Criticism,* 2:730.

8. In a note, Babbitt directs his readers to Goethe's review of Manzoni's *Conte di Carmagnola (Jubilaums Ausgabe,* vol. 37, 179–90), and remarks, "As a matter of fact Goethe has lifted the three questions bodily from the first paragraph of Manzoni's preface to this work" (*On Being Creative,* 29).

9. Wylie Sypher, "Irving Babbitt: A Reappraisal," *New England Quarterly* 14 (March 1941):64.

10. Hoeveler, *New Humanism,* 77.

11. Nevin, *Babbitt,* 39.

12. Ibid., 45.

13. Ibid., 46.

14. "The New Humanism," *Thinker* 2 (July 1930); reprinted in *Theodore Dreiser: A Selection of Uncollected Prose,* ed. Donald Pizer (Detroit: Wayne State University Press, 1977), 260.

15. *New Laokoon,* 122. He also says that "Judged by any standard Rousseau is a man of intellectual power" (145) and that his writings were "at least as assured of immortality as any of Voltaire's, and are at the same time filled with color and imagery" (148).

16. Fredric Jameson, *The Political Unconscious: Narrative as a Socially Symbolic Act* (Ithaca: Cornell University Press, 1981), 81.

17. Harry Salpeter, "Irving Babbitt; Calvinist," *Outlook and Independent* 155 (1930):422.

18. Northrop Frye, *Anatomy of Criticism: Four Essays* (New York: Atheneum, 1970), 33.

19. Ibid.

20. Ibid., 246.

21. Ibid., 247.

22. Jameson, *Political Unconscious*, 108.

23. Although most critics today regard Frye as a structuralist or a pre-structuralist, as Wimsatt and Brooks note, Frye "argues that literature, in so far as it is 'true to itself and its own character,' is concerned not to 'image life' but to 'commemorate some idea about it—or in other words to interpret it.' The interpretation that Frye demands is of a specific kind: it is not to be an economic or a sociological or an anthropological interpretation. It is to be a 'humane' interpretation, and for Frye this depends upon the 'new humanism' of Irving Babbitt and Paul Elmer More. Indeed, Frye's *Romance and Tragedy* must be regarded as one of the ablest documents produced by the New Humanists" (560).

24. Frye, *Anatomy*, 35.

25. Ibid., 41.

26. Austin Warren, "A Portrait of Irving Babbitt,' *Commonweal* 24 (1936):234.

27. Ibid.

Chapter Five

1. Richard Hofstadter, *Anti-intellectualism in American Life* (New York: Alfred Knopf, 1963), 405. For the account of Oates's address and the laxity of graduate work, see Samuel Eliot Morison, *Three Centuries of Harvard, 1636–1936* (Cambridge: Harvard University Press, 1936), 22.

2. Eliot, *Educational Reform*, 134. On Eliot's reforms, see Morison, *Three Centuries*, 323–99, and Frederick Rudolph, *The American College and University: A History* (New York: Random House, 1962), 287–306. Morison counters the charge that Eliot was a Rousseauist, his elective system being a way to shift from external to internal discipline even though many students would abuse their freedom (see p. 344).

3. Morison, *Three Centuries*, 369.

4. *LC*, 47, 53. Hereafter page references cited parenthetically in the text.

5. Eliot, *Reform*, 120.

6. Ann Douglas, *The Feminization of American Culture* (New York:

Alfred A. Knopf, 1977). See especially Part One, "The Sentimentalization of Status."

7. Quoted from Laurence R. Veysey, *The Emergence of the American University* (Chicago: University of Chicago Press, 1965), 222.

8. Noah Porter, *The American Colleges and the American Public,* 2d ed. (New York: Charles Scribner's Sons, 1878), 71; Hiram Corson, *The Aims of Literary Study* (New York: Macmillan & Co., 1895), 10, 28, 81, 13; Veysey, *American University,* 239; Gates quoted in Veysey, 239.

9. Ronald Story, *The Forging of an Aristocracy: Harvard & the Boston Upper Class, 1800–1870* (Middletown, Conn.: Wesleyan University Press, 1980), 166.

10. Lowell quoted from Morison, *Three Centuries,* 446. On Harvard's honors program, see Morison, 448–49.

11. "President Eliot and American Education," *Forum* 81 (January 1929): 4, 7.

12. For general dicussions of philosophical conservatism, see Clinton Rossiter, *Conservatism in America: The Thankless Persuasion,* 2d ed. rev. (New York: Random House, 1962), 3–66, and Ronald Lora, *Conservative Minds in America* (Chicago: Rand McNally & Co., 1971), 3–27.

13. David Spitz, *Patterns of Anti-Democratic Thought* (New York: Macmillan Co., 1949), 228–55.

14. Russell Kirk, *The Conservative Mind* (Chicago: Henry Regnery Co., 1953), 366.

15. "The Breakdown of Internationalism," *Nation* 100 (17 June 1915):679.

16. William E. Leuchtenburg, "Progressivism and Imperialism: The Progressive Movement and American Foreign Policy, 1898–1916," *Mississippi Valley Historical Review* 39 (December 1952):483–504; C. Roland Marchand, *The American Peace Movement and Social Reform, 1898–1918* (Princeton: Princeton University Press, 1972), xiii, 144–81.

17. John Milton Cooper, Jr., *The Warrior and the Priest: Woodrow Wilson and Theodore Roosevelt* (Cambridge: Belknap Press of Harvard University Press, 1983), 255.

18. Eric F. Goldman, *Rendezvous with Destiny: A History of Modern American Reform,* rev. ed. (New York: Random House, Vintage, 1977), 105.

19. See Richard Hofstadter, *The Age of Reform from Bryan to F.D.R.* (New York: Random House, 1955), 131–86.

20. Quoted from Cooper, *Warrior and Priest,* 128, 184.

21. Quoted from Hofstadter, *Age of Reform,* 179–80.

22. Nevin, *Babbitt,* 172 n. 71.

23. Aristotle, *Politics,* 1326b.

24. Donald K. Pickens, *Eugenics and the Progressives* (Nashville: Vanderbilt University Press, 1968), 16.

Chapter Six

1. G. R. Elliott to Babbitt, 26 September 1929, Babbitt papers; Norman Foerster, "Humanism and Religion," *Criterion* 9 (1929):26.
2. Quoted from Joseph M. Kitagawa, "The History of Religions (*Religionswissenschaft*) Then and Now," *The History of Religion*, 133.
3. "Buddha and the Occident," in *The Dhammapada*, trans. Irving Babbitt (New York: Oxford University Press, 1936); reprinted in *Irving Babbitt: Representative Writings*, ed. George A. Panichas (Lincoln: University of Nebraska Press, 1981), 234; hereafter cited parenthetically in the text as *D* followed by page number.
4. Friedrich Nietzsche, *The Will to Power*, trans. Walter Kaufman and R. J. Hollingdale (New York: Vintage, 1967), 270.
5. Martin Heidegger, *Nietzsche: The Will to Power as Art*, trans. David Farrell Krell (San Francisco: Harper and Row, 1979), 1:39.
6. Ibid., 73.
7. Babbitt to More, 12 June 1932.
8. More in *Man and Teacher*, 336.
9. Hoeveler, *New Humanism*, 176–77.
10. M. H. Abrams, *Natural Supernaturalism: Tradition and Revolution in Romantic Literature* (New York: W. W. Norton & Co., 1971), 65, 260.
11. William Blake, *Jerusalem*, in *The Complete Writings of William Blake*, ed. Geoffrey Keynes (London: Oxford University Press, 1966), chap. 1, pl. 4, 1. 23; chap. 4, pl. 98, 1. 39; and chap. 4, pl. 99, 11. 1 and 5. The interpretation of *Jerusalem* follows that of Northrop Frye, *Fearful Symmetry: A Study of William Blake* (1947; reprint, Princeton: Princeton University Press, 1969), 386, 390–91.
12. Frye, *Anatomy of Criticism*, 354.
13. More to Babbitt, 26 December 1923. Babbitt's comments on Sorel and Vaihinger are in undated reading notes in the Babbitt Papers. They were made in response to an April 1913 review of a book entitled *Vital Lies*, by Vernon Lee.
14. Thomas Nevin believes Babbitt possessed a Gallic mind contrasting with the more Germanic minds of Royce and most other American philosophers (*Babbitt*, 145). However, Thomas F. Powell sees a direct connection between the two men's conceptions of ethical work (*Josiah Royce* [1967; reprint, New York: Twayne Publishers, 1974], 108).
15. Josiah Royce, *The Philosophy of Loyalty*, in *The Basic Writings of Josiah Royce*, ed. John J. McDermott (Chicago: University of Chicago Press, 1969), 2: 932, 962.

16. Quoted from Powell, *Royce*, 108.

17. Samuel M. Osgood, *French Royalism Since 1870* (The Hague: Martinus Nijhoff, 1970), 106–23. For Babbitt's views on the *Action Française*, see the account by Marcus Selden Goldman in *Man and Teacher*, 234–35.

18. Quoted from Sydney E. Ahlstrom, *A Religious History of the American People* (New Haven and London: Yale University Press, 1972), 784. See 763–784 for an account of the rise of liberal theology.

19. Aristotle, *Nicomachean Ethics*, 1103a and 1104b.

20. Nevin, *Babbitt*, 142–43.

21. Paul Kurtz, ed., *Humanist Manifestos I and II* (Buffalo: Prometheus Books, 1973), 18.

22. Perry Miller, *The New England Mind: The Seventeenth Century* (Cambridge: Harvard University Press, 1939), 34.

Selected Bibliography

PRIMARY SOURCES

1. Critical Works (in chronological order)
Literature and the American College: Essays in Defense of the Humanities. Boston
    and New York: Houghton Mifflin, 1908. Reprint. Chicago: Gateway
    Editions, 1956; Clifton, N. J.: Augustus M. Kelly, 1972.
The New Laokoon: An Essay on the Confusion of the Arts. Boston and New
    York: Houghton Mifflin, 1910.
The Masters of Modern French Criticism. Boston and New York: Houghton
    Mifflin, 1912. Reprint. New York: Farrar, Straus & Co., 1963;
    Westport, Conn.: Greenwood Press, 1977.
Rousseau and Romanticism. Boston and New York: Houghton Mifflin, 1919.
    Reprint. New York: Meridian Books, 1955; Austin: University of
    Texas Press, 1977; New York: AMS Press, 1978.
Democracy and Leadership. Boston and New York: Houghton Mifflin, 1924.
    Reprint. Indianapolis: Liberty Classics, 1979.

2. Editions and Translations (in chronological order)
Zadig, and Other Stories, by Voltaire. Boston: D. C. Heath, 1905.
Racine's Phedre. Boston: D. C. Heath, 1910.
*The Dhammapada: Translated from the Pali with an Essay on Buddha and the
    Occident.* New York: Oxford University Press, 1936. Reprint. New
    York: New Directions, 1965.

3. Collections of Essays (in chronological order)
On Being Creative and Other Essays. Boston and New York: Houghton
    Mifflin, 1932. Reprint. New York: Biblo & Tannen, 1968.
Spanish Character and Other Essays. Edited by Frederick Manchester, Rachel
    Giese, and William F. Giese. Boston and New York: Houghton
    Mifflin, 1940. Includes a bibliography of all of Babbitt's published
    work, including anonymous reviews, and an index of names and topics
    covering Babbitt's critical books and the collections of essays.

4. Uncollected Essays

"The Breakdown of Internationalism." *Nation* 104 (17, 24 June 1915): 667–80, 704–6. Traces World War I back to the expansive individualism and sentimental humanitarianism of revolutionary France. Considers German oppression only as manifestations of a broad international movement.

"Humanism: An Essay at Definition." *Humanism and America*. Edited by Norman Foerster. New York: Farrar & Rinehart, 1930. Babbitt's effort to explain humanism as a practical way of life for the average person.

5. Selected Writings

Irving Babbitt: Representative Writings. Edited and introduction by George A. Panichas. Lincoln: University of Nebraska Press, 1981. Includes major essays and a good bibliography.

6. Unpublished and Miscellaneous Materials

Babbitt Papers. Harvard University Archives. Harvard University, Cambridge, Massachusetts. Contains a typescript of the Babbitt-More correspondence, lecture and reading notes, some letters, some financial records, and the manuscript of Babbitt's translation of the *Dhammapada*.

Harry Hayden Clark Papers. University of Wisconsin Archives, Madison, Wisconsin. Includes extensive notes of Babbitt's lectures in comparative literature.

Stuart Sherman Papers. University of Illinois Archives. University of Illinois at Urbana. Includes twenty-one letters from Babbitt.

SECONDARY SOURCES

1. Books and Parts of Books

Eliot, T. S. "The Humanism of Irving Babbitt." In his *Selected Essays*. 2d ed. New York: Harcourt, Brace & World, 1950. Sympathetic to humanism, but claims it tends to supplant rather than augment religion. In the same volume, "Francis Herbert Bradley" and "Second Thoughts about Humanism" provide valuable comments.

Foerster, Norman, ed. *Humanism and America: Essays on the Outlook of Modern Civilization.* New York: Farrar & Rinehart, 1930. Includes essays by Babbitt, More, Eliot, and several minor humanists.

Grattan, C. Hartley, ed. *The Critique of Humanism.* New York: Brewer & Warren, 1930. Too often polemical essays by some of Babbitt's contemporaries. The best are by Kenneth Burke, Allen Tate, and Yvor Winters.

Guttman, Allen. *The Conservative Tradition in America.* New York: Oxford University Press, 1967. Argues that Babbitt diverges from conservatism by refusing to embrace Christianity, a refusal that contributed to his later isolation.

Hoeveler, J. David. *The New Humanism: A Critique of Modern America.* Charlottesville: University of Virginia Press, 1977. Good summaries of the views of the main proponents of New Humanism. Also a good comparison of humanism to pragmatism.

Kazin, Alfred. "Liberals and New Humanists." In his *On Native Grounds.* New York: Harcourt, Brace & Co., 1942. A highly unsympathetic account that treats Babbitt as a commonplace Yankee Republican and Tory materialist who thought himself a Savonarola and who led some of his followers to fascism.

Kirk, Russell. "Critical Conservatism." In his *The Conservative Mind.* Chicago: University of Chicago Press, 1953. Reprint. New York: Avon, 1968. A brief and somewhat distorted view of Babbitt's politics. Considers Babbitt's thought the first full flowering of American conservatism.

Levin, Harry. "Irving Babbitt and the Teaching of Literature." In his *Refractions: Essays in Comparative Literature.* New York: Oxford University Press, 1966. One of the best single essays on Babbitt.

Lora, Ronald. *Conservative Minds in America.* Chicago: Rand McNally & Co., 1971. Considers humanism a bitter, recriminating offshoot of the genteel tradition. Provides a generally fair account of the humanist position but gives too much credence to the contention, expounded by Spitz, that Babbitt wanted an unchecked, all-powerful leader.

Manchester, Frederick, and Odell Shepard, eds. *Irving Babbitt, Man and Teacher.* New York: G. P. Putnam's Sons, 1941. A collection of tributes from Babbitt's former students.

Matthiessen, F. O. "Irving Babbitt." In his *The Responsibilities of the Critic: Essays and Reviews.* Edited by John Rackliffe. New York: Oxford University Press, 1952. A sympathetic although unenthusiastic assessment.

Mercier, Louis J. A. *The Challenge of Humanism: An Essay in Comparative Criticism.* New York and London: Oxford University Press, 1933.

————. *American Humanism and the New Age*. Milwaukee: Bruce Publishing, 1948. The sequel to *The Challenge of Humanism*. An attempt to forge a theistic humanism from Babbitt's principles.

Nevin, Thomas R. *Irving Babbitt: An Intellectual Study*. Chapel Hill and London: University of North Carolina Press, 1984. The only full-length critical study of Babbitt's philosophy. It includes a bibliographical essay. The best work on Babbitt to date.

Spitz, David. *Patterns of Anti-Democratic Thought*. New York: Macmillan, 1949. Fairly points out the impracticality of Babbitt's political theory but seriously misreads Babbitt by describing this theory as authoritarian and fascistic.

Veysey, Laurence R. "Rival Conceptions of the Higher Learning." In his *The Emergence of the American University*. Chicago: University of Chicago Press, 1965. Places Babbitt in the context of disputes over educational reform. Excellent for background but does not adequately distinguish Babbitt from less philosophical defenders of liberal culture.

2. Articles

Blackmur, R. P. "Humanism and Symbolic Imagination: Notes on Re-Reading Irving Babbitt." *Southern Review* 7 (1941):309–25. Reprinted in his *The Lion and the Honeycomb: Essays in Solicitude and Critique*. New York: Harcourt Brace, 1955; London: Methuen, 1956. A rather peevish and inaccurate critique of Babbitt's doctrine of the imagination.

Foerster, Norman. "Humanism and Religion." *Criterion* 9 (1929):23–32. Attempts to answer Eliot's concern about the relationship between humanism and religion (see above).

Hoeveler, J. David, Jr. "Babbitt and Contemporary Conservative Thought in America." *Modern Age* 28 (Spring/Summer, 1984):181–92. Claims that Babbitt's writings are the "first and perhaps most powerful formulation" of conservatism in this century.

Kariel, Henry S. "Democracy Limited: Irving Babbitt's Classicism." *Review of Politics* 13 (October 1951):430–440. Links Babbitt's theory of moral leadership and faith in the Supreme Court as a principle of stability with the conservative thought of his age but faults the humanists for not recognizing the instrumental role of government in encouraging diversity through education.

Leander, Folke. "Irving Babbitt and the Aestheticians." *Modern Age* 4 (Summer 1960):395–404. Summarizes Babbitt's theory of the imagination and typical misunderstandings of it.

Lovejoy, Arthur O. Review of *Rousseau and Romanticism*. *Modern Language Notes* 35 (May 1920):302–8. The source of the often-repeated contention that Babbitt's extremism in attacking romanticism is itself romantic.

Nickerson, Hoffman. "Irving Babbitt." *Criterion* 13 (January 1934):175–95. This memorial essay is an enthusiastic endorsement of Babbitt's principles from a conservative point of view.

Panichas, George A. "Babbitt and Religion." *Modern Age* 28 (Spring/ Summer 1984):169–80. A response to charges that Babbitt is antireligious.

—————. "The Critical Mission of Irving Babbitt." *Modern Age* 20 (1976):242–53. A revised version reprinted as the introduction to *Irving Babbitt: Representative Writings* (see above). A sympathetic but somewhat inaccurate account of Babbitt's humanism.

—————. "Irving Babbitt and Simone Weil." *Comparative Literature Studies* 15 (1978):177–92.

Russell, Frances. "The Romanticism of Irving Babbitt." *South Atlantic Quarterly* 32 (October 1933):399–411. Accuses Babbitt of nominalism and faulty logic.

Ryn, Claes E. "Babbitt and the Problem of Reality." *Modern Age* 28 (Spring/Summer 1984):156–68. An excellent analysis of Babbitt's views on the relationship between the will and the imagination.

—————. "The Humanism of Irving Babbitt Revisited." *Modern Age* 21 (Summer 1977):251–52. Argues cogently that Babbitt's humanism is compatible with religious belief.

Shafer, Robert. "What is Humanism?" *Virginia Quarterly Review* 6 (1930):199–209. An inadequate attempt to expand Babbitt's distinction between humanism and humanitarianism.

Sypher, Wylie. "Irving Babbitt: A Reappraisal." *New England Quarterly* 14 (March 1941):64–76. Argues that Babbitt's ethics were dynamic but his aesthetics were formulaic.

Index

Abrams, M. H., 133
Action Française, 138
Adams, John, 112
Adamson Act, 127
Agrarians, Southern, 77–78, 118
Aiken, Conrad, 58
American Academy of Arts and Letters, 72
American Mercury, The, 72
Amherst College, 62, 108
antinomialism, 47
Anti-Saloon League, 127
Antoinnette, Marie, 118
aristocracy, 19, 20, 103, 115–16, 128, 141
Aristotle, 19, 30, 37, 38, 55, 59, 63, 64, 74, 90, 91, 92, 93, 95: Poetics, 97; Nichomachean Ethics, 12, 140
Arnold, Matthew, 19, 109, 117: Culture and Anarchy, 12–13

Babbitt, Albert, 4
Babbitt, Augusta Darling, 3
Babbitt, Bessie, 4, 15
Babbitt, Dora Drew, 25, 26, 65, 75
Babbitt, Edward S., 25, 26
Babbitt, Edwin, 3, 4, 6–10, 12, 13, 15
Babbitt, Esther, 25, 26
Babbitt, Irving, childhood and rootless early life, 3–4; classicism, 9, 12–13; composition, method of, 65–66; convention and social rituals as source of happiness, 25–26; conversion to humanism, 1, 11–15, 19; dialectical mind, 20, 122; eclecticism, 10, 16–17, 18, 59; education, 3–4, 10–15, 16–17; human law, search for, 107; humanist education, efforts to promote at Harvard, 111–12; marriage and family life, 25–26; masculine vs. feminine attitude towards life, 2, 5–6, 10–11, 18, 20, 21, 24; in education, 106–107, 109; New Humanists, leadership of, 1, 24, 60–62, 64, 75–78; philosophical disagreements with, 73–74; newspaper reporter, summer as, 4, 10; philology and philogists, attitudes toward, 15, 16, 18, 19, 21, 59, 105, 107; promotion and tenure at Harvard, struggles for, 21–24; prose style,

circularity and aphoristic basis of, 65–67;. Puritan heritage, 2–3, 6; reputation, 72–73; romanticism, early traits of, 9, 11; satirical intentions in books, 68–70; spiritualism, early belief in, 10, 12; stoicism during final illness, 26–27; strategies for spreading humanism, 62–64; teaching methods, 15, 21–22, 58–61; travels during college year abroad, 11–12

WORKS: BOOKS:
Democracy and Leadership, 66, 78, 112–28, 131, 140
Literature and the American College, 2, 20, 22–23, 63, 68–70, 78, 102, 104–11, 137, 138
Masters of Modern French Criticism, The, 30, 102
New Laokoon, The, 23, 37, 44, 82, 98–99
On Being Creative and Other Essays, 34, 93
Rousseau and Romanticism, 26, 31, 32, 53, 55, 71, 87, 140

WORKS: ESSAYS:
"Buddha and the Occident," 130–31, 139
"Humanism: An Essay at Definition," 75
"Interpreting India to the West," 65
"Rational Study of the Classics, The," 13, 108

Babbitt, Katherine, 3
Babbitt, Thomas, 3, 5
Bacon, Francis, 9, 59, 68, 69, 104, 105, 107, 115, 125, 135, 140
Bandler, Bernard, 71
Barth, John, 88–89: Sabbatical, 89; Giles Goat-Boy, 92
Barton, Bruce: Man Nobody Knew, The, 65
Baudelaire, Pierre Charles, 69, 74, 81
Bauer, F. C.: Das Manichäische Religionssystem, 18
beauty, 84, 85–90
Benda, Julien, 41
Blake, William, 55–56: Jerusalem, 135–36
Bôcher, Ferdinand, 20, 21
Boileau-Despréaux, Nicolas, 68

162

Bolshevism, 128; *See also* Marxism
Bookman, The, 71
Bowdoin College, 62
Brandeis, Louis, 123
Brody, Alter, 72
Brooks, Cleanth: *Literary Criticism,* 80
Brooks, Van Wyck, 58
Bryan, W. J., 66
Bryn Mawr College, 21
Buddha, 7, 12, 17, 19, 39, 64, 93, 113–
14, 115, 130–33, 136: *Dhammapada,* 17,
130
Buddhism, 10, 12, 17–18, 59, 63–64,
130–133, 139
Burke, Edmund, 67, 112, 117
Butterworth, A. P., 11

Caligula, 138
Canby, Henry Seidel, 76
Carlyle, Thomas, 14, 22
Carnegie Endowment for International Peace,
121
Carnegie Hall, 76, 77
Castiglione, Baldassare, 70
catharsis, 92–93
Catholicism, 128, 138
Cheever, John, 88–89: *Falconer,* 89
Chicago, University of, 23, 70
Christ, *See* Jesus
Christianity, 1, 10, 120, 127, 129, 130,
133–136; *See also* Catholicism, Protestant-
ism, humanitarianism, Social Gospel, Je-
sus
Coleridge, Samuel Taylor, 22, 82
Collins, Seward, 71, 72
Communist Labor Party, 124
Communist Party, American, 124
competition, 115–116, 122, 123
Confucianism, 114, 120
Confucius, 7, 39, 59, 93, 113, 114, 116;
See also Confucianism
conservatism, 1, 100, 112, 118
convention, 26, 35–36, 49–50, 51, 116,
139; *See also* habit
Cooper, James Fenimore, 28
Copeland, Charles Townsend, 22, 107
Corson, Hiram, 108, 109
Crane, Ronald S., 79
Crane, Stephen, 62
Criterion, 72
Critique of Humanism, The, 76
Croce, Benedetto, 47
Cummings, E. E., 58

Dante: *Divine Comedy,* 14, 17, 133, 135
Darling, Lucius, 3, 4–5
Darwinism, 61, 106, 107–108, 120, 127–
28, 139
decorum, 1, 36–37
democracy, 6, 19, 116, 118, 121, 122,
123, 124, 127, 128
Dewey, John, 112, 116, 140
Diderot, Denis, 97
dilettantism, 107
Dionysius of Helicarnassus, 59
Don Juan, 77
Dooley, Patrick Kiaran: *Pragmaticism as Hu-
manism,* 32
Dos Passos, John, 87: *Manhattan Transfer,*
72
Douglas, Ann, 2, 107
Dreiser, Theodore, 61, 87: *An American
Tragedy,* 88
dualism, 18–19, 44–48

Edwards, Jonathan, *28–30*
Einstein, Albert, 64
elán vital, 46, 118, 119, 121, 125
Eliade, Mircea, 130
Eliot, Charles William, 13, 20, 21, 22,
103–6, 107–8, 112, 121: "The New Ed-
ucation," 104
Eliot, T. S., 39, 59, 61, 72, 74, 75, 80,
129; *For Lancelot Andrewes,* 74; "Tradition
and the Individual Talent," 61; *Waste
Land, The,* 61
Elliott, G. R., 62, 75, 129, 138, 139
Emerson, Ralph Waldo, 8, *30–31,* 66, 69:
"Self-Reliance," 27, 135
Erasmus, Desiderius, 76, 112
eugenics, 128

Farrar and Rinehart, 76
fascism, 72, 125, 128, 138
Fichte, Johann Gottlieb, 50
Foerster, Norman, 61, 75, 76, 129, 130,
138, 139: *American Criticism,* 75; *Future of
the Liberal Arts College, The,* 61; *Humanism
and America,* 64, 76, 77; *Towards Standards,* 61
Ford, Henry, 65
Ford, J. D. M., 24
form, 81–82, 84, 98
formalism, 80–81, 83
France, Anatole, 30
freedom, *See* will, freedom of
frein vital, 46, 113, 117, 118, 119, 138

French Institute, 73
French Revolution, 67, 121, 123
Freudianism, 62, 93, 94
Frye, Hall, 62
Frye, Northrop, 97–98: *Anatomy of Criticism,*
   97, 136; *Romance and Tragedy,* 153n23

Gates, Merrill, 108
genius, 30, 86
genre, 82, *96–101*
Giese, William, 10, 11, 12, 21, 23, 26
Goethe, von, Johann Wolfgang, 30, 55, 83–
   84, 89–90
golden mean, 1, 9, 12; *See also* mediation
Gompers, Samuel, 127
Goodwin, William Watson, 14
grace, 1, 28–29, 40–41, 95, 129, 133,
   137, 141
Grandgent, Charles H., 21

Habegger, Alfred: *Gender, Fantasy, and Real-
   ism in American Literature,* 143n6
habit, 139–41
Hall, G. Stanley, 14
Harding, Warren G., 124
Harriman, E. H., 110, 112
Harvard University, 4, 6, 10–11, 13, 19,
   20, 21, 22, 23, 58, 60, 66, 73, 103–
   104, 105, 106, 107, 110–11, 123
Hawkes, John, 88–89: *Second Skin,* 89
Hazlitt, Henry, 42
Hegel, Georg Wilhelm Friedrich, 48, 137
Heidegger, Martin, 99–100, 131
Heraclitus, 130
higher will, *See* will, higher
Hinduism, 10, 73
Hirsch, E. D., 101
history, 51–52, 91, 95, 120–21, 135
Hobbes, Thomas, 113
Hoeveler, David, 87, 133
Hofstadter, Richard, 104
Horace, 4, 68
Hound and the Horn, The, 71
Huerta, Victoriano, 123
Hugo, Victor, 69
Humanism and America, See Foerster, Norman
humanitarianism, 9, 19, 23, 36, 45, 68–69,
   113, 119, 127, 139, 141
humility, 114, 121, 130, 131–32, 139
Huxley, Aldous, 88

I'll Take My Stand, 77–78
Illinois, University of, 24, 61

imagination, 17, 38, 42, 43, 44, 86, 91,
   95, 118, 125, 141
Imagism, 62
imitation, 37, *90–96,* 109, *113–114,* 117,
   118, 125, 139
imperialism, 71, 113, 121, 122, 124, 127
individualism, 112–113, 114, 123, 128,
   137, 138, 140
inner check, 43

Jackson, Andrew, 122
James, Henry, 88
James, William, *31–33: Principles of Psychol-
   ogy, 33; Will to Believe, The,* 31; *Varieties
   of Religious Experience, The,* 32
Jameson, Fredric, 91, 98
Jefferson, Thomas, 122
Jesus, 39, 40, 66, 93, 113, 114, 117, 127,
   138, 139
Johnson, Samuel, 22, 44, 67, 68
justice, 113, 115, 116, 124, 127
Juvenal, 69

Kant, Immanuel, 47, 91: *Critique of Aesthetic
   Judgment,* 85
Kazin, Alfred, 78
Keats, John, 60, 107
Kenyon College, 4
Kernan, Alvin, 69
Kirk, Russell, 118
Kittredge, George Lyman, 14–15, 58, 70
Krutch, Joseph Wood: *Modern Temper, The,*
   77

labor unions, 116, 126–27, 136
Lamartine, de, Alphonse Marie Louis, 77
Lasserre, Pierre, 138
law, human, 119–120, 128, 131–32; *See
   also* Nemesis; measure, law of
League of Nations, 116
League to Enforce Peace, 122
Lenin, Nikolai, 125
Lessing, Gotthold, Ephraim, 99
Lévi, Sylvain, 16
Lewis, Sinclair: *Main Street,* 68
libido: dominandi, 120, 121, 125, 126, 128,
   131, 138; *sciendi,* 120, 125; *sentiendi,* 120;
   See also will to power
Lincoln, Abraham, 112, 118, 122
Lippmann, Walter, 58
Locke, John, 115
London, Jack, 2, 88
Longinus, Dionysius Cassius, 59

Lowell, A. Lawrence, 23, 24, 111
lust, See *libido*

Maag, William, 58
McDougal, William, 126
Machiavelli, Niccolo di Bernardo, 74
Marcou, Philippe Belknap, 21
Marraus, Charles, 138
Marshall, John, 112, 118
Marx, Karl, 115
Marxism, 91–92, 120
Masters, Edgar Lee: *Spoon River Anthology,* 68
Mather, Frank, 19
measure, law of, 40, 41, 44
mediation, 48, 49, 56–57, 118, 124, 132–33, 134, 140
meditation, 132,–33, 139, 140
mélange des genres, 84, 96, 100
Mencken, H. L., 1, 2, 68, 72, 93
Mercier, Louis J. A.: *Mouvement Humaniste aux États-Unis,* 75
Miller, Perry, 141
Modern Language Association, 77
modernism, 63–64; *See also* positivism, science
Mohammedanism, 10
Molière, 121
monism, 8, 44–45, 47, 49, 91
Montaigne, de, Michel Eyquem, Seigneur, 109
Montana, College of, 15–16, 104
More, Louis Trenchard, 64
More, Paul Elmer, 1, *18–19,* 21, 22, 23, 24, 26, 48, 61, 62, 63, 65, 66, 68, 71, 72, 73, 74, 75, 78, 87, 129, 133, 136, 138, 139: *Demon of the Absolute, The,* 64
Mozart, Wolfgang Amadeus, 25
Munsterberg, Hugo, 106, 109, 110
Mussolini, Benito, 72, 125

Napolean Bonaparte, 122
Nation, The, 23, 24, 72
National Institute of Arts and Letters, 72
naturalism, 8, 140; *See also* monism
Nemesis, 119–20, 128
Nero, 138
Nevin, Thomas, 30, 52, 62, 87, 88, 141
New Humanism, The, 1, 19, *71–78*
New Republic, The, 72
Niebuhr, H. Richard, 139
Nietzsche, Friedrich Wilhelm, 121: *Will to Power, The,* 131
Nineteenth Century and After, The, 75

Norris, Frank, 87, 88
Northwestern University, 65
Norton, Charles Eliot, 14–15, 17, *19–20,* 22, 108, 110
Novak, Michael, 129
Novalis, 50

Oakes, Urian, 104
One and the Many, 30, 85, 119, 130, 132, 136
originality, 87

pacificism, 122
Panichas, George A., 1
paradox, classical and romantic, 50
Parmenides, 130
Pascal, Blaise, 52–53, 108
Percy, Walker, 88–89: *Lancelot,* 89
Perry, Bliss, 58
Petrarch, Francesco, 69
Plato, 12, 19, 63, 73, 74, 113, 116, 130, 131
Poe, Edgar Allan, 48
Pope, Alexander, 68
Porter, Noah, 108, 109
positivism, 43
Pound, Ezra, 64
Pound, Roscoe, 123–24
pragmatism, 132; *See also,* James, William
Princeton University, 73
Progressivism, 62, 112, 122, 124, 127, 128
Protestantism, 129, 138–39
psychology, 63–64, 103, *109–10,* 119, 122, 125, *130–33,* 139, 140; *See also libido,* Freudianism
Puritanism, 6, 65, 76, 104, 111, 117–18, 119, 122, 140, 141

racism, 125–26
Radcliffe College, 21, 25
Ransom, John Crowe, 77: *World's Body, The,* 80
Raphael, 115
Reed, John, 58
relativism, 59, 83
Renan, Ernest, 59, 102
restraint, 116, 122; *See also frein vital*
Ricardo, David, 115
Robespierre, de, Maximilien François Marie Isidore, 122
Rockefeller, John D., 110, 112
romanticism, 1, 60, 133–34; *See also* Rousseauism

Roosevelt, Theodore, 2, 5, 123, 126
Ross, Edward A.: *Old World in the New, The,* 126
Rousseau, Jean-Jaques, 9, 30, 45, 59, 68, 69, 70, 89, 104, 105, 107, 122, 134, 135, 137
Rousseauism, 115, 120, 140; *See also* romanticism
Royce, Josiah, 25, 73, *137–38: Philosophy of Loyalty, The,* 137–38
Ruskin, John, 14, 48
Rymer, Thomas, 69
Ryn, Claes E., 37, 38, 43

Sainte-Beuve, Charles Augustin, 30, 54, 91
Salpeter, Harry, 96, 99
Saturday Review of Literature, 76
Schiller, von, Johann Chistoph Friedrich, 48, 85, 86
Schlegel, Friedrich, 50
Schofield, William Henry, 59
science, 1, 8, 13–14, 17–18, 63–64, 107, 129, *130–32; See also libido sciendi*
secular humanism, 141
Shakespeare, William: *Hamlet,* 15
Shelley, Percy Bysshe, 60, 107
Shepard, Odell, 77
Sherman, Stuart Pratt, 22, 24, 74, 139: *Matthew Arnold,* 61; *On Contemporary Literature,* 61
Shorey, Paul, 23
Shun, 116
Sinclair, Upton, 72, 87
Smith, Adam, 115
Social Darwinism, *See* Darwinism
Social Gospel, 127
socialism, 62, 121
Socrates, 7, 51, 54–55, 93, 117
Socratic method, 12, 117
Sophocles: *Oedipus Rex,* 92
Sorel, George, 136
Spencer, Herbert, 127
Spencer, Theodore, 76
Spengler, Oswald, 120
Spingarn, J. E.: *Creative Criticism,* 71, 83–84

Spiritualism, 7, 8, 133
standards, *34–37,* 114, 122, 125, 137; *See also* symbols, imagination
Stevens, Wallace, 58
Stoddard, Lothrop: *Rising Tide of Color, The,* 126
Sumichrast, de, Frederick Caesar, 21
Sumner, William Graham, 127
Supreme Court, 117, 123
Swedenborg, Emanuel, 7
Swift, Jonathan, 70
symbols, 78, 118, 120, 138; *See also* imagination, standards, imitation

Tate, Allen, 42, 77
Taylor, Frederick W., 105
tradition, 33, 61, 64, 107
Transcendentalism, 7; *See also* Emerson, Ralph Waldo
Twain, Mark: *Huckleberry Finn,* 134

Vaihinger, Hans: *Philosophy of As-If, The,* 136
Van Doren, Carl, 76
Veysey, Laurence R., 108

Wagner, Richard: *Die Walküre,* 93
Warren, Austin, 1, 60–61, 101
Warren, Robert Penn, 77
Washington, George, 112, 118
Wendell, Barrett, 107
Whitehead, Alfred North, 64
Whitman, Walt: "Song of Myself," 138
will, freedom of, 12, 38, 47, 63–64, 86, 113, 126; general, 121; higher, 34, 37–*44,* 86, 94, 120, 125, 129, 131, 135, 137–38, 140, 141; *See also* will to power
will to power, 45, 123, 127, 131; *See also libido dominandi*
Williams College, 20
Wilson, Edmund, 26, 72
Wilson, Woodrow, 122–23, 124, 127
Wimsatt, W. K., 67: *Literary Criticism,* 80
World Court, 116
work, hierarchy of, 114–15, 126, 127, 138